PUTNAM'S HANDBOOK OF EXPRESSION

PUTNAM'S HANDBOOK OF EXPRESSION

FOR THE ENRICHMENT OF CONVERSATION, WRITING, AND PUBLIC SPEAKING

COMPILED by

EDWIN HAMLIN CARR

GYAN

Published by

GYAN

Gyan Publishing House
5, Ansari Road
Daryaganj, New Delhi-110002
Phone: 011-47034999, 9811692060
E-mail: books@gyanbooks.com

Distribution Network
gyanbooks.com
India, USA, Canada, UK, Australia, France

ISBN : 978-81-212-6022-0 (PB)
First Published, 1915

2nd Impression 2021

Printed at: Gyan Press, Delhi.

Putnam's Handbook of Expression
Compiled by: Edwin Hamlin Carr

Putnam's Handbook of Expression

For the Enrichment of Conversation, Writing, and Public Speaking

Compiled by

Edwin Hamlin Carr

G. P. Putnam's Sons

New York London

The Knickerbocker Press

The Knickerbocker Press, New York

To

Any Person Who Recognizes Herein One of His Own Original Phrases

Foreword

FOREWORD

So far as I know, there is no book which is distinctively a phrase book. Because of this fact, I have for years been collecting phrases from all sources. Whenever and wherever I have found in any volume, magazine, newspaper, or during conversation, a distinctive phrase I have made a note of it.

This volume is the result of an endeavor to classify these phrases so that the reader may secure a synonymous phrase as, in a book of synonyms, he secures a synonymous word.

It would be difficult for me to give credit for every phrase found in this book. In fact, it would be impossible to determine who are the authors of the larger number of our English phrases. I have, however, found in certain books a number of phrases so distinctive and characteristic that it is only proper to give due credit to the authors.

The novels of Dumas have supplied a great number of phrases for conversation, and I have found good material also in the correspondence of Mrs. Hannah More.

Foreword

Many general phrases have been derived from the writings of Thackeray, and the Essays of Samuel McCord Crothers.

For sermonic phrases I have found the writings of the Rev. Thomas Guthrie, D.D., and the Rev. J. H. Jowett, D.D., particularly helpful.

Men who have ability to make new phrases may be pleased to have at hand a book of this kind.

The clergyman who begins his every observation with "It seems to me" and continues "Along that line," will find here a variety of prefatory and introductory phrases.

Teachers who make a habit of adding new words and new phrases to their speech will doubtless find good browsing here.

There is perhaps no more difficult letter to write than one of condolence. A number of phrases are given under this designation, in order to assist in this most difficult and yet most blessed task.

Since we talk in phrases as well as in words, every home needs a phrase book as well as a dictionary.

I wish to make grateful acknowledgment to James Baldwin, author of *The Book Lover*, and to Miss Isobel Stevenson, of the New York City Public Library, for valuable suggestions concerning the arrangement of the book, and to Prof. Charles Knapp, of Barnard College, New York City, for assistance concerning the Foreign Phrases.

E. H. C.

Using the Phrases

USING THE PHRASES

The entire volume should be perused for phrases which appeal to one's taste. These should be marked and memorized, and it will be noticed that they will spring spontaneously to the lips or pen.

A suggestion for a determined effort to use the phrases may be found in R. L. Stevenson's practice of inventing a conversation. He says in his *Vailima Letters*, vol. i., p. 105:

"Though I write so little, I pass all my hours of field-work in continual converse and imaginary correspondence. I scarce pull up a weed, but I invent a sentence on the matter to yourself; it does not get written; but the intent is there, and for me (in some sort) the companionship. To-day, for instance, we had a great talk. I was toiling, the sweat dripping from my nose, in the hot fit after a squall of rain: methought you asked me—frankly, was I happy. Happy (said I); I was only happy once; that was at Hyères."

Contents

CONTENTS

Contents

Contents

Contents

I

Phrases for Conversation

Complimentary of Things

COMPLIMENTARY OF THINGS

How delightfully cozy
This is the sort of thing I enjoy
I like the idea very much
That's simply splendid
There is an unfailing charm in it
A delightful idea truly
I like it prodigiously
Is n't that jolly
It bears the stamp of excellence
It is worthy of high praise
Of first-rate merit
I was highly pleased with it
It was in the best taste
It is worthy of a world of praise
It is a beautiful piece of industrial accomplish-
ment
I call it a delightful spectacle
A capital idea
Altogether a fine thing
A sentiment worthy of emulation
A source of constant pleasure
A very real asset
With none of the slight faults of immaturity

It is an uplifting habit
The sight filled me with admiration
Of no ordinary cleverness
It was perfectly splendid
It is a fine instance of
It called forth unqualified admiration
It was strikingly impressive
The result exceeded my most sanguine expectations
The finest flower that ever blossomed
It is an amiable habit by no means to be discouraged

CORDIALITY

I am delighted to make your acquaintance, though indeed I seem to know a great deal about you through
I am looking forward to having a good talk with you
It is a great pleasure to me to welcome you
I am very impatient to learn how you are progressing
You are most welcome, I was expecting you
How happy we are to see you, you have become almost a stranger to us
I must have a chat with you soon

Courtesy

I am delighted to see you here
It is a great pleasure to have met you
I would be delighted to talk with you but unfortunately I am very hurried
I trust we shall soon meet again
I warmly regret being unable to oblige you
I am mightily glad to see you

COURTESY

Kindly convey my warmest regards to
I beg your acceptance of my very hearty thanks for
Be so good as to present my most respectful compliments to
You are most kind
Please do not give yourself that trouble
I am delighted to have your approbation
Tell him that we will do ourselves the pleasure of calling on him
You anticipate my wishes
I thank you very much
I have great pleasure in being useful to you
You are very obliging
Permit me to thank you
I wish you a pleasant journey
On the contrary, I ought to thank you very heartily

Conversation

Please accept this as a slight token of my gratitude

I hope my coming will not put you to any inconvenience

I wish you a safe and pleasant journey

I trust I shall have an opportunity of returning your kindness

I beg you to excuse me

I am sorry it is not in my power

I am very sorry I cannot assist you

I offer my most sincere apology

I wish you good morning

I want to thank you for all your kindness

I am much improved in health, I thank you

Pardon my indiscretion

I do not know how to respond to such kindness,

The only recompense I can make you is good will

I thank you for the compliment

I hope you enjoy your usual health

How did he bear his misfortune

I hope you will favor us with a call

Tell me some more particulars

May I give you some assistance

Does the game of —— please your fancy

May I have the honor of your company

May I ask whether

Will you do me the kindness to

Will you do me the favor to tell me

Conventional—Apologetic

Is not this a characteristic of
How do you understand it
What has procured me so flattering a distinction
To whom is he indebted for the place
Aren't you going
Did you say that you were there
I thank you for your kind inquiries
Don't let me detain you for doubtless you have engagements

CONVENTIONAL—AT WEDDINGS

I wish you much joy
Let me wish you every happiness
I wish to offer you my heartiest congratulations
I congratulate you heartily on the good fortune that is yours to-day
Kindly accept my sincerest good wishes
It is impossible to wish you any greater good fortune than you have had to-day
Please accept my congratulations
Hearty congratulations

CONVENTIONAL—APOLOGETIC

I must apologize for my stupidity
This is quite unforgivable, I fear
I am very awkward, pray forgive me

I beg you will excuse me
I regret that I cannot assist you
It is with no small regret that
I am exceedingly sorry that your request comes to me at a time when I am so pressed by my own affairs, that I cannot, with any convenience, comply with it
I offer my most sincere apology
Pardon my indiscretion

CONVENTIONAL—CONDOLENCE

Kindly accept my sincere esteem and sympathy
I beg to offer my profound sympathy
We all share in your loss, and you have my deepest sympathy
I sympathize with you in your great affliction
I wish to assure you of my heartfelt sympathy
I could not refrain from assuring you in person of my sincerest sympathy
We can all splendidly trust God in life, no matter what its vicissitudes, if we but feel that we are drawn nearer to Him
Please accept my sincere condolences

CONVENTIONAL—ON LEAVING A HOST

This has been a delightful occasion
This has been a most enjoyable evening

Conventional—Being Introduced

I am under the greatest obligation to you for a charming evening

I have enjoyed this little glimpse of you very much

This has been a most agreeable experience

It has been delightful to have you with us

I hope you may be persuaded to come again

I wish you were not going quite so soon

Come to see us again before you leave town

I trust you will repeat this experience at some future date

I want to make my parting compliments

CONVENTIONAL—ON BEING INTRODUCED

I am very happy to meet you

It is a great pleasure to meet you

I am delighted to know you

I am sure the pleasure is mine also

I was not clever enough to catch your name

Thank you, I appreciate your kindly thought of me

It has been a great pleasure to have met you

I am delighted to make your acquaintance, though indeed I seem to know a great deal about you through

You are most kind

It is a great pleasure

It is good of you to say so

CONGRATULATORY

I cannot refrain from expressing my admiring appreciation of

You are to be congratulated upon the

I wish to congraulate you, and express my appreciation of

Will you permit me to make an acknowledgment of appreciation to you for

Permit me to make appreciative acknowledgments of

Please accept my congratulations upon your

Since the news of the joy that has happened to you reached me, I have been anxious to write you a word of congratulation

I congratulate you on the very fortunate opportunity which presents itself

I had the great pleasure of hearing that

I take this opportunity of assuring you that

It is with great pleasure I hear of your safe arrival

COMMENDATORY OF PERSONS

He is a perpetual surprise even to those who know him best

She is a charming person to set people at their ease

He is a noble character

Commendatory of Persons

She talked beautifully
He is a man of many fascinations
He has a fine face full of vigor
He is very patient and very brave
We have beautiful neighbors
I never have seen you looking in better health
You are looking as lovely as usual
They form a delightful group
How lovely these are
With him there is little seeking after effect
I always thought the hour struck sooner in your home than anywhere else
It is an evidence of good breeding
He possesses the rare faculty of
She is without a shadow of affectation
He is incapable of hurting any one's feelings
He possesses a masterly understanding of the subject
You have a very helpful suggestion
He is irresistibly funny
He is uncommonly quick
He has a genuine aptitude for business
A man whose merit equals his reputation
He acquitted himself admirably
He possesses a good deal of homely dignity
He has the talent of dispensing pleasure
He is finely qualified by exceptional educational advantages

Conversation

She is a very tender and indulgent mother
He is full of generous sympathies
He has considerable colloquial talents
He has a sunny temperament
He is quite an adroit flatterer
He seems to have an inexhaustible supply of affection
His modesty is worthy of wide imitation
He is brimming over with new ideas
He gives you a jolly shake of the hand
He has a wonderful gift of making friends
He has a circle of interesting friends
There is something very likable about him
He is truly regardful of the interests of others
He cultivates the amenities and civilities
He understands the art of making allowances
He would shun to break the bounds of courtesy
His polite best
He is above the meanness of tale-bearing
He spoke in language clear and expressive in the highest degree
He spoke with his accustomed felicity of language
It was a very neat and appropriate expression
He labored in a simple and straightforward manner to
He possesses nerves that seem to be of iron

Commendatory of Persons

He is one who can do the thinking for a commonwealth
He has a character of sterling excellence
He is of consequence in the world
She is a model of propriety
There is an indefinable charm about her
He has an air of businesslike decisiveness
He is a facile talker
He is a plain frugal man
He is untinged by prejudice
He has a taste for polite conversation
He discharged his difficult task admirably
He was actuated by the most laudable motives
He never fumbles
He is always in such perfect good humor
He behaved very handsomely
He has calm good sense
He did it with good grace
He fitted his environment perfectly
You could not apply to any one better able than he
He made a most delightful impression
He is chock-full of fine sentiment
My heart warms toward him
He is a person whom I always recall with pleasure
His letters are full of heartiness
He has such a kindly and sympathetic spirit

Conversation

He is every whit a man's man
He has fine manners
He acted as one to the manor born
May his tribe increase
He impressed me prodigiously
He has the highest ideals of fine, clean, strong manhood
She is possessed with the most delicate intuitions
He possesses a certain suavity of manner
She is of exceptional personal beauty
He is above the average in point of conversation
He took the hugest pains to accommodate us
There is no more noble and beautiful character than she
There was something captivating in his manner
He was eloquent without being declamatory
You will go a long way before you find a better man

CRITICAL OF PERSONS

He is a rather crabbed specimen of humanity
He gives me qualms
He is insufferably tiresome

Critical of Persons

I would as soon take Beelzebub himself into my plans

I can nowise explain what sort of whim, prank, or perversity it was that induced him to act thus

Unhappily one is so fettered by

What utter bosh it all is for him to

He is bereft of his senses

He is a selfish, graceless thankless person

He is insufferably mean

He is an odious old reprobate

He makes such idiotic excuses

His appearance is peculiarly forbidding

You will receive the passport to disfavor if you

He is in constant danger of becoming mean and sordid

We are not all of that ilk

The suspicion arises in at least some minds, that the reprehensible art of lying has several practitioners in this country

Men who scold and whine, and prophesy ill

He is not able to get the right perspective

We are quite reluctant to follow his lead

He has no ground of complaint

He will have about his ears a unanimous chorus of derision and bitterness

He presented a series of lame apologies

He is in no small degree responsible for

Conversation

He is exceedingly dull
He cuts a sorry figure
His manner lacks sincerity without which no one can be truly agreeable
He is the prey of every passing circumstance
He is positively without a spark of humor
He is ponderously dull
He lapsed into arrant triviality
He emphasizes the defects
He has a great propensity for running into debt
He fails to see the need of making plentiful provision
His message might have been more fitly worded
He has no sense of the fitness of things
More foolish words were never spoken in reply to a serious argument
His conclusions are hopelessly detached from his premises
He is quite incapable of generous sentiments
The real difficulty against which he has butted head down is
I am in a critical spirit
The theory has gone into bankruptcy
It is cheap and ignorant talk
He is stupidly over-confident
I asked him how he could vindicate such an enormity
He is a derelict of mankind

Critical of Persons

He is an acrimonious critic
He has the baneful habit of
He is a mere bungler
He has a desert in his mind
He is apt to be malicious
He has a sullen and uncommunicable disposition
A man who never had a taste or emotion but what was sordid
He is over-quick in reproof
He richly deserves his fate
A village pest
More nice than wise
An insufferable bore
A wearisome grumbler
A devilish insinuating way of
A most inadequate notion of
Altogether discreditable
I will not use terms of endearment
He takes himself and his cause always with equal seriousness
Equally bad
He is handling the affair with a mixture of supineness and imbecility
He follows the line of least resistance
He unwittingly plays into the hands of the enemy
He is full of moral cowardice and dissimulation

Conversation

He lives in his little provincial world
He has never given a hint of practical value
He is always whimpering for help
His thoughts are always vague and ill-defined
He is a lazy, lolling sort of human
That was a sensible admonition directed against
his silly talk
He is charged with exaggeration if not willful
distortion of the facts of the case

DISSENT

I protested in vain
It would simply freeze my blood if
I was awakened for the first time to its full significance when
In which case I should remonstrate
It is enough to turn one's brain
That's the very thing I complain of
What hurt my feelings was that nothing I could
say would do any good
It is monstrous
It is shocking
The very heart and soul of justice have been
plucked out of her unresisting carcass
It is a stupid thing to do, to my mind, and I
don't see the point
It is preposterous

Dissent

It's absurd
I remonstrated at the time
It is certainly not a very pleasant thing to
  think that
I cannot refrain from expressing my regret
  that
I am distracted with the cares of
It is really heartbreaking to see
It is very annoying to me
I can scarcely credit it
The uncertainty is irritating
It puts me in a decidedly awkward position
He gave no very gracious consent
I fervently hope not
Decidedly not
Figures don't lie, but often they do not speak
  plain enough to be understood at the
  first hearing
You can ill afford to
I loathe it
I was exceedingly mortified that
He might have sat for a picture of insensibility
I assure you such is not the case
It is scarcely worth raising our heads to look at
I was nervous at the thought of it
There is danger of an embarrassing rupture
He was not slow in expressing his disgust at the
  conduct of

Conversation

I care not a fig who knows it
It is a sore thing for me to have to do this
Heaven forbid that such a thing should come
    to pass
I know precisely what it signifies
I think it would be quite inadvisable to do so
He could out-slang the boldest bargeman
The pitiful thing about it all is
It is a manifest absurdity
It is in a bad way
The statement is the merest nonsense
The latest and most absurd theory is
I hate, abhor, sicken at it
I want most emphatically to disclaim any in-
    tention of

INQUIRY

What course shall you take to get your money?
What do you know of his history?
Where shall I be likely to find him?
What has he there?
have: you any news?
What kind of man is he?
When do you leave?
Where do you intend to settle?
Have you had luncheon?
May I have an apple?

Prefatory

Will you obey me?
Have you had any tidings of your brother?
What did you observe?
In what part of the country do you live?
Where are you staying?
We spent an agreeable evening together.

PREFATORY

As luck would have it, I ,
To be candid, I
It seems a positive calamity that
Do you seriously imagine that
No one could be so rash as to assert that
I am satisfied that
I strongly suspect that
I fancy that
Further than this
Paradoxical as it may seem
I dare say that
It is with great pleasure that
It would ill become me to remark that
For instance
The redeeming feature of it all is
Quite by chance, I
I have been wondering whether
In all probability we
It is not likely that

Conversation

Luckily I
It is a singular coincidence that
I took particular pains to notice whether
It is with problems such as these that
How very fortunate it is that
It is a particular piece of good fortune that he
As a matter of fact
None the less, I
It can be admitted too that
Certain it is that
In some quarters it is believed that
If that be the case, I
I confess I look with some alarm at
I have the great good fortune to have heard that
I realize afresh that
The art of arts is
I flatter myself that
It is from the heart that I can request that
I am perfectly convinced that
The full gravity of the situation is seen in the fact that
Regardless of any thing I said
I am painfully conscious that
I wasn't by any means sure I
It dawned upon him gradually that
It is seldom that

Prefatory

We may be quite sure that
I have repeatedly said that
It cannot but carry with it instant conviction
    that
By some mischance, I
Prior to this, we
I was greatly elated to find that
I am heartily glad that
I know the nicest little secret
I had a happy thought to-day
I cannot but realize that
It is scarcely conceivable that
Frankly, I
It is intellectually unthinkable that
On the other hand
I appreciate most deeply the
I am devoutly thankful for
At all events
None the less
Hitherto
Furthermore
Further than that
Nevertheless
Notwithstanding
In the meantime
Frequently the
In all candor
I rather apprehend that

Conversation

I have sometimes thought that
It must be owned too, that
I scarcely feel as if I
I rather imagine that
To this day I hardly know whether I
A very striking proof of the fact is
I will hazard the observation that
On the other hand
You have made me curious. Tell me of it
I have news for you
May I give you an instance
It is quite indifferent to me whether I
He used frequently to observe that
What is the explanation? It is simplicity itself
Now that I am a little seasoned I
I have heard him often lament that
You may guess what luck
I regret extremely that
It would have been quite out of the question for us to
Recently I came across this
I was about to inquire what you thought of
I have the deepest veneration for
He has conceived the happy idea of
I suppose the inference we are expected to draw is
I am confident of one thing that

Prefatory

My principal motive for acting thus was
I am fully aware that
I perceive, moreover, that
It is surely true that
I marvel that
I sometimes fancy that
I humbly conceive that
I apprehend that
Of course, I am perfectly aware that
I presume that
There are pretty certain indications that
It often amazes me that
It seems hardly probable that
I affirm that
I have the consolation to hope that
It is still permitted us to hope that
It would be futile to deny that
It is reasonable to assume that
There is no prospect that
In these circumstances it
I suppose that
I warrant that
I confess I am not indifferent to
I shrink instinctively from
I confess a less and less relish for
I am impatient and querulous under
It is a sort of presumption to expect that
I cannot imagine to myself

Conversation

I have a kindly yearning toward
I heartily approve of
I do not advert to
I have long believed that
It has long been the fashion to
I have been falsely assuring everybody that
One cannot help noticing that
There are plenty of evidences that
The difference, I take it, is this
The fact of the matter is
If I rightly remember
It is a just cause for praise that
It was a happy circumstance for me that
I wish with all my heart that
I am grateful to find that
I devoutly wish it may prove to be that he
It is not to be supposed that
My attention has been directed to the
I have a mental reservation with regard to
A very affecting circumstance happened yesterday
I have a story worth telling
I had the rare distinction of
I had a very civil note from
If I may hazard a conjecture, I should rather think
It was unusual for me to
He seems to be obsessed with the idea that

Prefatory

There is but a thousand-to-one chance that
It is an open secret that
I have an impression that
I informed you wrongly when I said that
If I mistake not, I believe that
If I may use the expression I think that
Quite regardless of my remark, you
I had the inexpressible comfort of knowing that
He made a touching proof of his regard by
I flatter myself that
Is it not a great mercy to have such a helper?
Again and again, I
Inadvertently, I
I felt like uttering a mild disclaimer when
I have little predilection for
I had the rare satisfaction of
I was strangely moved when I heard that
There is a certain distinctive advantage in
I was amazed to find that
In my poor judgment, I
I hold in all seriousness that
Has the tide of victory set in your favor?
By what magic have you found out the secrets of
We have plumed ourselves upon our ability to

Conversation

RESPONSE

It is good of you to say so
He is to be most warmly felicitated
I have fallen into splendid hands
How nicely you put that
How lovely of you
Those friends of yours are delightful people
He is able to extract comfort and pleasure out of
hard experiences
You decide rightly
I was received with the utmost kindness
I am quite delighted
Permit me to compliment you
How consoling you are
I was never more entertained
You got out of that rather neatly
It is like talking the art of war before Hannibal
I quite agree with you
Very luckily for me
You have not guessed rightly
With all my heart
We acquiesce
That tends to confirm my opinion
I will make ample allowance
Don't give way to such a fancy
How unfortunate
I am glad to hear such good tidings of

Response

I am a sort of amateur Father-Confessor, you know
I am not as strong as I fancied myself
A very extraordinary measure I confess
A day that I still recall with pleasure
We haggled about the price
I fear I cannot go
Surely none of us would relish such treatment
He deems it well worth while
I can make a guess as to the probable results
I think it is about time to tincture our ideals with common sense
It is most refreshing
You have rightly judged
She was strangely diffident
He responded so good-naturedly
He should be highly thankful
Our effort was futile enough
Very rarely
Quite likely
Unquestionably
We have ample time
Quite frequently
It is all the most ardent supporter could wish
Fortunately there is still a more excellent way
I'm afraid he started the day in a contradictory mood
He is never very closely confined to the facts

Conversation

It is a sore trial to his temper
The paper gives a beggarly account of the affair
I think I can do it without danger of reprobation
I am trying to help him compose his difficulties
He did it in all good faith
I had the simple satisfaction of knowing that
He is suffering from a confusion of ideas
The exceptions are so few as to be negligible
It is not expedient for us to do otherwise
It was too sore a subject for levity
I reciprocate your good wishes
The matter was brought to a satisfactory termination
It was real stupid of me
It completely surpasses my comprehension
It caused me a thousand apprehensions
The odds seem overwhelmingly against them
I think she is a wee bit jealous
He is a miserable victim of anxiety
I am afraid he will be taught by many a sore and scalding lesson
It is decidedly humorous
I am open to suggestion
It would neither remove nor confirm my doubts
I hate all ostentation
Upon subsequent occasions he was very affable

Response

Heaven knows how or when
If they could be convinced it would be a godsend
Much to our profit and delight
It is the only possible course
Not that I know
I do not wish for any
It is a matter of no importance
He is sick but not in danger
He is in feeble health
We suffered great hardships
Hād I known it, I
I do not remember
I will summon him
I should have liked very much to have seen him
I have seen him
I admit you've provocation for it
I cannot recollect
I have finished
I assure you he was very much astonished
Thank you for your cheering words
You give me more credit than I deserve
Forgive me all my delinquencies
I cannot find words to express the intense pleasure I have always in
I appreciate keenly the favor you have shown me
It was delightful I assure you
It is really a pleasure to assist you

Conversation

You have great reason to congratulate yourself on
I supposed that it was he whom you meant
I supposed it to be me whom you meant
I do not know that I can. I wish I were able to
I should not have intruded on you at this hour
You would do me such a service I could scarce repay
With pleasure
I am quite delighted
I am ardently wishing for it
I imagine it must have been he
I am not sure I rightly understand
I am happy to think so
Yes, I quite understand how it happened
Fortunately so
We were fortunate enough to find one
I wish it were true
I was taken aback for the moment
Receive my sincere congratulations
I am delighted to hear you say so
I am most grateful to you
Most assuredly
It was very thoughtful of you
I feel indebted for your kindness
I will rejoin you directly
It would be the culmination of my fondest hopes to see

Response

I should think it to be very much to one's advantage to
A pleasant coincidence happened recently of which I must tell you
Be that as it may, I
If the truth must be told, I
It is nothing less than marvelous that
I exerted myself much to make him cheerful
He was inflexible to all entreaty
I am not at all solicitous about it
It is not very conspicuous
I acquiesce
Certain unforeseen emergencies arose to hinder me
In spite of statements to the contrary I think that
In the long run, I
One can be thankful enough for
I hope your anticipations will be realized
I had gratifying success
In no manner of way
Of the finest sort
Its plausibility cannot be denied
I intend to gratify my curiosity some day
He has the unhappy knack of saying things that are not so
I can give no adequate explanation of it
I feel amply repaid for my effort

Conversation

We consider it a huge joke
It was a matter of no consequence
That is really interesting
The news is decidedly reassuring
It is most extraordinary
It was altogether delightful
It is exceptionally good
The result exceeded my fondest expectations
We were delighted beyond measure
Bless your heart, yes
I am entirely callous
I feel that I have no more backbone than a jellyfish
That is far from being the whole truth
This merits reflection
Indeed, to a refreshing degree
I will endeavor to be strictly impartial
I am luckily disengaged to-day
I confess that there is something very sensible about that view
What you tell me is simply astounding
At present there is no indication of such a millennium
I have been inexorable to all invitations
Certain unforeseen emergencies arose to hinder me
I suspect you know all about it
I think his course is very unjustifiable

Response

I do not doubt that he will be here
He expects to get off to-morrow
I regard him as being the cleverest man of my
acquaintance
He has given them no pecuniary assistance for
some time
His affairs are in a bad condition
He fled the city
It is nothing else than agreed
We happened to be present on the occasion
He is a man of small means
I purpose leaving for home in the morning
He would not believe but that I did it
She is a widowed woman
It was a long discussion
I will go no farther
I have nothing further to say
I met a rather agreeable woman at dinner
A lady, a friend of mine, told me
I have asked two or three ladies and several men
I expect two or three gentlemen
It has been a delightfully agreeable day
This is a fine morning
I have neither eaten nor drunk anything to-day
It looks as if it would rain
This is the largest of all I have seen
That kind of apples is best
We are likely to have a fine day

You are quite right
It is so gratifying to me
How splendid it is in this connection that
She will return presently

TACTFUL RESPONSE

Now, as they say, you are asking me a question
I am accustomed to that appellation
It will afford us much food for reflection
It is a fine thing to be open to conviction
I wait events
It is well worth looking into
The matter is not past mending
I will reflect upon it
I am hopelessly old-fashioned in some things
I am very tranquil about it
It is too remote for reminiscence
He spoke very sparingly of the occasion
It is a fascinating field for difference of opinion
Ask me something easy
I am neutral
The deponent sayeth not
The problem is surely most perplexing
I think, perhaps, there might be a happy medium
It is surely a point of view novel enough to
merit attention

Tactful Response

There seems no very great diversity in our sentiments
I often wish things were otherwise
I am not inclined to tinker with it
It seems that it is a case difficult either of proof or disproof
The question is surely a thorny and complex one
I am open to suggestion
What part of Ireland are you from?
Isn't that a sad state of affairs
I wish to act in consonance with the beliefs that I have so long adhered to
Give me your opinion of

II

General Phrases for Speech and Writing

Commendatory of Things

CONVERSATION

A desire to excel in speech and expression.
Unable to express himself with any degree of force or fluency in conversation
A good converser
A condensed verbal statement
The art of conversation
The immortal Socrates taught by conversation alone
The luxury of talk
An eloquent, fascinating talker
A man whose genius shone in conversation
He charmed everybody he met by his talk
He fused the thoughts of others into his own
A suggestive talker
The charm of conversation
Brilliant conversation
A felicitous talker

COMMENDATORY OF THINGS

A very promising beginning
A delight to all right-minded people
A work of unique value

The finest thought the human mind can cherish
A master-stroke of policy
A task of immense interest
Big with promise
A most excellent speculation
It is the ideal method of solving the problem
An asset of incomparable value
With new and increased capacities
A very pretty problem in
An experiment of absorbing interest
In the most fetching style
It has much to commend it to the sober judgment of thinking men

CRITICAL OF THINGS

Pure cussedness
Superficially clever
Notions that will not bear the world's scrutiny
I feel quite inspired to doubt the accuracy of
Decidedly dreary
In a very maudlin state
Entirely without qualifications
Highly improper
Unhappily rare nowadays
A clumsy attempt
A lame effort

Critical of Things

A distinction without a difference
Not beyond just criticism
A miserable poverty-stricken mental attitude
Absurdly out of place
Little to charm the eye
Ingenious but hardly convincing
An invincible ignorance
With few tokens of affluence
A stoic callousness
A very tame and spiritless thing
With no serious responsibility
Slipshod methods
A little pusillanimous motive
They neutralize a large part of their effort by
A foolish shortsighted policy
A slight indiscretion
A rather monotonous life
A man lays himself open to criticism by
An unfortunate notion
Mentally deficient
A stingy curmudgeon
It is a situation to be lamented
Not altogether a wise thing to do
The first source of confusion is
There is a shade of uncertainty in
There is a distressing dearth of
I have a strong foreboding that
It is a silly piece of business

Speech and Writing

An event which I shall always remember with unpleasant recollections
There exists a morbid condition of dissatisfaction
It presents an ugly aspect
There is no general unanimity of opinion
It is an abnormal condition
A fly in the ointment
There is an obvious lack of sympathetic understanding
Statements which are positively alarming
Nothing could be more reprehensible
Such is the ingratitude of man
One of those pitiless rebukes
The disastrous effect is too plain to admit of any argument
The very name appears a fatuity
A narrow scrutiny that robs the act of its natural charm
Not the most reassuring thing in the world
Nothing is more annoying than
An error worse than heresy
It is not possible to describe in decent language the
Spiteful rivals whisper that
A condition that must be met without delay
The rude jostle of our selfish existence
With the most perfect indifference
It is an evidence of vulgarity of sentiment

Critical of Things

A creature of impulse
The revival of an old humbug
A slight mist of uncertainty
Which really means nothing when you look squarely at it
Agitated by useless disputes
A suggestion to be taken with reserve
An idle meaningless pastime
It is devoutly to be hoped that
It is the quintessence of hypocrisy
It is but the legitimate offspring of his policy
They are a forlorn lot
It is a vital mistake
In this unseemly manner
It comes with senile decay
Without a moment's remorse
A custom which has properly been abolished
Nothing could be worse, speaking within the limitations of human imagination, than
The false and the actual
You never saw such an air of ruin and bankruptcy as everything wore
A theory which has sins enough of its own to answer for
They receive more attention than their small wit will justify
A shameful and infamous practice, meriting the contempt and scorn of all real gentlemen

DESCRIPTIVE OF PERSONS

A matchless eye
A winning smile
With feminine ease and grace
A very pretty manner
A finely molded chin
A great lubberly boy
A black, chubby, kinky-haired pickaninny
A chubby-handed, ruby-lipped baby
A maid of winning charm
A most winsome expression
A dainty little miss
A mere slip of a girl
Nimbly moving hands
In robust health
In her smartest evening suit
A husky youngster
A tar of the jolly old sort
A son frightfully dissipated
An officer immensely officious
The habit of gentle speech
The habit of accurate observation
The pink of perfection
A vast amount of good sense
A superior man
An obliging person
A magnanimous soul

Descriptive of Persons

A good-natured fellow
A most agreeable creature
A natural sweetness of disposition
A charmingly simple person
A quiet unassuming person
A man of sound sense
A man of immovable convictions
A lawyer of marked ability
A discriminating eye
A countenance which beautifully expressed a deep interest in all things good
A well-governed mind
With the intuitive perceptions of a lover
Many charming qualities
A heart alive to all the beauties of nature
With the most fastidious punctuality
Fond of dwelling on the scenes of other days
So frankly and innocently happy
Skilled in the graces of conversation
An unsympathetic reader
A man of dignity, force, and ease of manner
A decent pride
A clear brain
A flash of intelligence
A quick sympathy
A wise tolerance
An acute observer

A splendid fellow
A very mercenary person
A trustworthy friend
A fond mother
A good listener
An excellent musician
An exceptional man
A character worth knowing
A mind of penetrating keenness
A scholar of considerable eminence

DESCRIPTIVE OF THINGS

A lovely landscape
A quiet nook
A crimson rosebud
A fertile region
A drowsy drone
A snug farm
A dainty flower
The blissful skies
Serene weather
The most perfect night possible
In very picturesque surroundings
A charming aspect
A rugged background
A high-crested crag

Determination

A pool of transparent clearness
The kindly fruits of the earth
The most appetizing confection
The pleasing odor of good food
A delicious condiment
A deadly contagion
A munificent gift
Snowy table-linen
The boundless beauty of springtime
The blissful skies
A rattling good story
A savory odor
A quaint old house
Of a make quite metropolitan
A suit of faultless cut
Delicate traceries
A facile pen
A nice omelet

DETERMINATION

Downright mulishness
With an air of stolid desperation
With unflinching determination
Not to be tempted into foolhardiness
He held on with grim determination
With determined perseverance
Gently but firmly

A vigorous determination
With stoical fortitude
With all the energy of one's soul
With redoubled energy
Consumed by the intensity of a passion for
A quiet determination to do their part nobly
A grim endurance
Struggling with circumstances
With indomitable patience
He has a phenomenal capacity for pegging away
Not swerved from his position by a hair's breadth
In proportion to the strength and persistency of an intelligent effort
Pretty persistently
He is disputing the crown of his profession with his neighbor
I warm to a man who has gall in his liver
He gave us a clear and vigorous presentation of his own position
With indomitable spirit
With unremitting assiduity
Unsubdued in spirit and undepressed in mind
A grim hold upon
An obtuse human
A persistent tendency to

ENERGY

An enthusiastic ardor
A dash of recklessness
With fervent aspiration after
My spirit fired at such indignities
An eager disputant
In fine fettle
An alert and inquisitive mind
Fired with enthusiasm for
With surprising dexterity
A new impetus
Notable and far-reaching activities
The real spice of what would be otherwise prosaic and dull
Into the stir and hubbub of the world
A stirring place
With bewildering rapidity
With tremendous earnestness
Called into action by a new emergency
Strained almost to the limit
Their efforts were happily crowned with success
He gave himself without stint
A mighty dynamic
Ginger and go
Vigorous and hot for the fray
Firmness and strength underlying
The habit of stoutly claiming our rights

Cling with all the tenacity you can muster
A great deal of perseverance is needed
Able to bear the brunt
A matter of great necessity
The limitations of human endurance
At pains to give a wide circulation to
A decided tendency toward
He labored with the utmost intelligence and energy
We need to accentuate some phases of
He placed his business on an excellent footing
No other so piquant instance
A brimming tide of energy
A stout-hearted people
A fountain of boundless energy
The overflow of energy
With considerable energy
With the air of finality
In pretty constant activity
Prodigiously active
An emotion which impels to action
A strenuous life
Never relaxing
Intent on getting a comfortable livelihood

EGOTISTIC

Overbearing arrogance
The pride of singularity

Figurative

He has a very high opinion of himself
Naturally self-contained
His vanity was delicately tickled
He is captivated by a sense of his own importance
She came in with insufferable condescension
With a sort of bravado
In a very supercilious manner
With a surly grunt of recognition
A few curt remarks
All the grist must be ground through his mill
He proceeded with the greatest gusto to
With sulky acquiescence
Reticent and self-contained
An affected civility

FIGURATIVE

Like a young rose in summer time
As sullen as an ill-tempered boy
As acid as vinegar
Like a thousand silent years
As impressible as wax
Like a watch with an inelastic spring
His heart as heavy as lead within him
As brown and supple as a hazel twig
As pitiless as pestilence
As fierce as flame
Wrinkled as an old parchment

Speech and Writing

Trembling like an aspen leaf
Like the precision and grace of a sea wave
Like fine-spun cobwebs, with greedy puffed-up, spider-like lusts in the middle
As idle as a painted ship upon a painted ocean
As full of good-fellowship as a sugar-maple is of sap
Like a live red-hearted volcano
Like a ruby gem on a wristlet of steel
It is like trying to use a large screw driver to turn a small screw
As for man his days are as grass
My heart palpitated like a trip hammer
Like the restless tides of the ocean
As helpless as animals driven to slaughter
The righteous shall flourish like the palm tree
With Niagara-like impetus
Like the homeward instinct of the bee
It vanished like snow falling in the river
The form changed like a chameleon
Like the last echo born of a great cry
Like flies upon a festering sore
As black as ebony
As white as snow
As thin as a shadow
As flat as a flounder
As sharp as a needle
As smooth as glass

Figurative

As slippery as an eel
As rough as a bear
As still as a statue
As fierce as a tiger
As changeable as the moon
As burning as the thirst of the fever-stricken
As old as the moon
As impressible as wax to the seal
As graceful as Apollo
As obsolete as croquet
Like a salt sea-mist
Like slender palms along the oasis
Like little foxes among the tender vines
Like a dozing aged man
Drifting like an idle straw at the mercy of the
wind
As gloomy as an old man by a fireless hearth
Like the slowly fading light of the sun at evening
As heavy and clumsy as a bear
As tired as a weary traveler on the burning
sands
Like the sighing of autumn winds
As tall and stately as a poplar tree
As delicious as a breath of heaven
Like the sunny eyes of a baby
As beautiful as apple blossoms in an orchard
Rang through my heart as joy-bells fill the air
As bald as a cannon-ball

Looked as fresh as a rose
As happy as an angel
As weak as water
A face like a wooden face
Like a sea of glory
As naturally as perfume distills from a rose
As sweet as angel-dreams
Like the beating of a mother's heart when her child is saved
Clinging like a blight to the souls of men
Swift as a shadow
Short as a dream
As thrilled as a débutante at her first ball
As envenomed as an asp
Like a beautiful rose of rare fragrance
Like a drowsily clinging bee on a clover-head
As distant as the farthest star
As cheerless as the Arctic Circle
As sweet as a song on a summer's eve
As easily as one could mend a spider's web
As instinctively as some can read love in the heart of a rose
Like a huge python winding round and round its victim
Jet-black as ravens' wings
As tedious as a twice-told tale
As tedious as a tired horse

Figurative

As clear as a whistle
Like a sunbeam on a winter's day
It froze all the fountains of love
The fragile thread of life
Smothered under the wet blanket of
The deeps of degradation
A hazy sea of memories
A cat-like circumspection
Reaping a dragon-tooth harvest
The echo of a disappointed soul
His mind cankers
They froze me to silence
Such a snore as the nose of innocence can produce
A touch of languor in the air
A work too hard for the teeth of time
The gulf of oblivion
Robbed of our tranquillity
Sick with vanity
In the twinkling of an eye
The tents of wickedness
The lion's share
Leaven that is gradually purifying the world
A rose-buddy sort of
Weaves into the fabric of memory silver threads
To bind with chains of gold
Skating on thin ice
Galvanizing substitutes

Speech and Writing

The perilous undertow of
It will come out in the wash
Blasted with eternal barrenness
The weary treadmill of the established system
More polite than a duchess
Limping with weariness
A world swarming with engagements
Swifter than a weaver's shuttle
Clearer than the noonday
Broader than the sea
As the stars of heaven for multitude
Like a wave of the sea driven with the wind and
tossed
A land flowing with milk and honey
Like a spring whose waters cannot fail
Empty of the kernel of good sense
Like a doddering old woman
The dew of thy youth
Sown broadcast over the whole region
The seamy side of life
A flight of fancy
A lull in business
The thread of existence
Salt that keeps civilization from decay
The last dregs of reality
It becomes impossible to nurse their wrath
Like a river that wanders and widens and waters
many fields

Figurative

Like a whirlpool which seeks its own center
Robbed of its heritage
A bottomless sea of speculation
He doesn't care a broken egg-shell for her
Like an inconsiderate boy
Diamonds as large as pigeon eggs
Earrings like chandeliers
It clings like a burr
A tower of strength
The salt of the earth
The light of the world
The wings of the morning
Like a jewel in a swine's snout
Honey-combed with heresy'
The lance that unhorses every one is
Well rooted in the garden of memory
I am the lonely slave of an oft-wandering
    mind
I hear the roll of the ages
Age will chink the face
He has climbed to the snows of age
An age of gold
Like a quiet mind in a loud world
A bevy of apple-cheeked girls
The bitter springs of anger and fear
The spawning place of crime, ignorance, and
    debauchery
Still in its mewling and babbling infancy

Feeds on the swine-husks of
Through all these laggard stepping years
Urged to blow a stimulating blast upon
In a stage whisper
As fascinating as a romance
A mind of the steel-trap order
He has shown good marksmanship in shooting folly as it flies
He took the bit in his teeth and ran away with the
The community is like your grandmother's button bag
Driven like a leaf before the wind
Like clipped currency, not worth its full value
Like a dead flower with beauty and fragrance fled
Under the lash of
As well founded as the law of gravitation
The sun of his life sets in a blaze of glory
Milder than any mother to a sick child
Shrouded in mystery
A sleep like the first sleep after torture
Black as if cast from the shadow of a fallen angel's wing
As much as plants need sunshine
As wax to receive impressions
As steel to retain impressions

FOREIGN—LATIN

Ad captandum vulgus, to catch the rabble
Argumentum ad hominen, an appeal to passion rather than to reason
Ad infinitum, endlessly
Ad interim, in the meanwhile
Ad libitum, at pleasure
Ad nauseam, to disgust
Ad rem, to the point
Ad valorem, according to the value
A fortiori, all the more surely
Alma mater, fostering mother
Alter idem, another precisely similar
Anno Domini, in the year of our Lord
A posteriori, from facts back to principles
A priori, from principles to facts
Bona fide, in good faith
Cui bono? for whose good
De facto, on the basis of facts
De novo, anew
Deo gratias, thanks to God
Deo volente, with God's consent
De profundis, out of the depths
Dramatis personae, the actors in a play
Ecce homo, behold the man
E pluribus unum, one composed of many
Ergo, therefore

Esto perpetua, let it endure forever
Et cetera, and so on
Ex cathedra, with high authority
Ex officio, by virtue of his office
Ex parte, partisan
Ex post facto, after the deed is done
Ex tempore, on the impulse of the moment
Gloria in excelsis, Glory in the highest
Ibidem, in the same place
Ibid, in the same place
Id est, that is
Idem, the same
Item, also
In articulo mortis, at the point of death
In hoc signo vinces, under this standard thou shalt conquer
In medias res, in the midst of things
In memoriam, in memory
In perpetuum, forever
In re, in the matter of
In statu quo, in the former state
In toto, completely
In transitu, in passing
Ipsissima verba, the very words
Ipso facto, by virtue of that very fact
Jubilate Deo, rejoice in the Lord
Jus gentium, the law of nations
Lapsus linguae, a slip of the tongue

Lis pendens, the pending suit
Magnum opus, a great work
Mala fide, treacherously
Meum et tuum, mine and thine
Mirabile dictu, strange to say
Modus operandi, manner of operation
Multum in parvo, much in little
Ne plus ultra, perfection itself
Nil desperandum, no need to despair
Nolens volens, whether he will or not
Labor omnia vincit, labor overcomes every difficulty
Non sequitur, it does not follow
Nota bene, mark well
Omnes, all
Paterfamilias, the head of a household
Pater noster, Our Father
Particeps criminis, a sharer in the crime
Peccavi, I have erred
Per annum, by the year
Per capita, by the head
Per centum, by the hundred
Per contra, contrariwise
Per diem, by the day
Per se, in itself
Pro bono publico, for the public good
Pro et con, for and against
Pro tempore, for the time being

Quantum libet, as much as you please
Quid pro quo, a substitute
Quod vide, which see
Requiescat in pace, peace to his ashes
Scripsit, he wrote it
Semper felix, always fortunate
Semper fidelis, always faithful
Semper idem, always the same
Seriatim, in sequence
Sine cura, without care
Sine die, without a day appointed
Sine qua non, an indispensable prerequisite
Status quo, the current situation
Sub rosa, secretly
Sui generis, unique
Summum bonum, the highest form of virtue
Tempus fugit, time flies
Terra firma, the solid earth
Terra incognita, an unknown country
Tuum est, it is your own
Una voce, unanimously
Ut infra, as stated below
Ut supra, as stated above
Verbatim, word for word
Versus, against
Via, by the way of
Vice versa, the terms being exchanged
Vi et armis, by main force

Viva voce, orally
Vox populi est vox Dei, the voice of the people is the voice of God

FOREIGN—FRENCH

À la mode, according to the style
À outrance, without mercy
Au fait, up to the mark
Au reste, besides
Au revoir, adieu until we meet again
Beau monde, the fashionable world
Bête noire, a pet aversion
Bonhomie, good nature
Bon jour, good morning
Bonne bouche, a delicate morsel
Bon soir, good evening
Chapeaux bas, hats off
Chef de cuisine, head cook
Contretemps, an awkward situation
De trop, out of place
Edition de luxe, a splendid edition
En déshabillé, in undress
Enfin, finally
En masse, in a body
En rapport, in harmony
En route, on the way
Entre nous, between ourselves

Esprit de corps, the animating spirit of a collective body
Faux pas, a mistake
Hors de combat, down and out
Laissez faire, let things take their natural course
Lèse-majesté, high treason
Ma chère, my dear
Ma foi, on my honor
Mal à propos, ill-timed
Mal de mer, seasickness
Mon ami, my friend
Noblesse oblige, rank imposes obligations
On dit, they say
Par excellence, preëminently
Peu à peu, by degrees
Raison d'état, a reason of state
Robe de chambre, a morning gown
Sans souci, free from care
Tout ensemble, the general effect

IRRITATION

A fit of nervous exasperation
Evidences of a reckless temper
An unpleasant passage of words
Impatient of delay
Exasperated beyond expression
Much piqued

Manly

Acting with the petulance of a child
Irritably self-conscious
Angry at the most minute provocation
Driven into nervous prostration
Thin-skinned in the presence of annoyances
Enough to imperil the habit of studied moderation of statement
The most exasperating of all nuisances
I was in the worst possible temper with
Irritability that has some justification
I never before have known anything so provoking
He used most vigorous terms in referring to
She hides all her vexation in her bosom
An error of the most exasperating sort
He is easily irritated
With the most astonishing perverseness
A weight of nerves without a mind
A few hot and bitter words
In utter exasperation

MANLY

Men who love their fellow-men and prove their love by service
He did not once deviate from his principles
He has a profound contempt for show and humbug

Men broad-brained and broad-shouldered for the task
Men of breadth of outlook
Men who foresee great things
Large-hearted and clear-eyed men
Real leaders
Men who keep in the straight path of duty
Every man shall bear his own burden
Men whose fidelity merits the highest praise
Men who would dare hell-heat or Arctic cold
Men whose intentions were never open to honest doubt
A man whose happiness was in serving others
Strong men
Untinged by prejudice
Clouded by no unfriendliness
Without acrimony
With no preconceived theories
In whole-hearted simplicity
Above suspicion
With entire frankness
No feeling of estrangement
A gleam of friendly light
The right mental attitude
The right hand of fellowship
In the sunshine of a genial nature
In the genial glow of the firelight
Of gentle mien

Most entertaining
The contagion of noble lives

MILITARISTIC

The zone of hostilities
The harmless victims of war
The strongest reason for a rupture among the nations
Tactical retreat
Martial enthusiasm
A crack regiment
Universal disarmament
Strict neutrality
The inevitable horrors of war
A military advantage
The war-makers of Europe
The ruthlessness of war
The neutrality of nations
Far from the ignoble strife of men
The futility of war as a means of settling disputes
The international equivalent of the policeman's club
Cannon fodder
The lust of empire
The cruel indignities of war
The long-nurtured passions of a nation

When the thunders of war are heard around the world
The arbitrament of arms
A test of materialism
An age crammed with war
The federation of the world
The policy of military preparedness
The patriotism of the common people
A military tattoo in the streets
The dominant military power in the world
The nightmare menace of war
The crime of Cain multiplied a million fold
The widespread sentiment for neutrality
The maintenance of peace
The menace of a world war
A sin against civilization
The stunning sense of some great calamity
The futility of militarism
The theater of hostilities
Needless, useless, wicked, wanton war
The allied armies
The pitiful misery of the people
A long-drawn-out conflict
An overwhelming numerical superiority
An appalling cost of human life
The diplomatic corps
A compact front
Wanton destruction

Opposition

Military necessity
Deliberate and wanton vandalism
With ruthless hand
The guilty madness of war
The inveterate belligerence of
A crushing indictment of Twentieth Century civilization
It only serves to inflame murderous thoughts of revenge
The city tense with the excitement due to militarism
Imbued with the spirit of war
Prepared for vigorous operations
Under cover of the artillery
The oft-trodden battle-ground of the Low Countries
A warless world
War is bad, unconscionably, irredeemably bad
An armed peace
The mailed fist
A religion of valor
The terrorism of military might

OPPOSITION

A good stout protest
A railing accusation
A storm of protest

It is out of the question
In perpetual protest
Stubborn resistance
A decided negative
In the face of mighty passions and desires
In the teeth of clenched antagonisms
It is time to protest and to protest vigorously
Not under any circumstances
Too heavily handicapped
A disposition in some to resent
A combination of hindrances
Without flinching
An insuperable barrier

OPTIMISTIC

I have nothing dismal to remember
A happy earnest life
Without grudge or grumbling
A hopeful attitude
An attitude of assurance
An inborn belief in the superiority of
Always hailed with joy
Quickening and cheerful influences
Assuredly we shall win
Of splendid augury
The habit of expectancy
A hopeful prospect

Optimistic

A promising beginning on intelligent lines
It is bound to accomplish a world of good
A brisk cheerful sense of things present and things to come
Some cheerful hope-laden ideas
No gloomy forebodings
We will have the fun of beginning again
An abiding optimism
With high expectations
Not a lurking doubt or suspicion lingers
The most hopeful sign of the times is
I know nothing more pleasant than to
This is indeed good fortune
How pleasant it is to
I have had a great piece of luck
Let us turn to more pleasant reflections
But, after all, in this as in everything else one must be hopeful
Unquestioned confidence
Without the least misgiving
It is an assured success
Conscious of being able to cope with the situation
Genuine confidence
It is in no wise inimical to your interests
To believe him guilty of deliberate mendacity would be painful
With undiminished confidence

A place of peace and unfailing cheeriness
A cheery greeting
In high glee
With many a cheering smile
He manifests a cheerful willingness
Deeply and unfeignedly happy
It is a cheerful sign of progress when
He is capable of taking the highest view which the circumstances of the case may admit
He has the habit of holding an expectant attitude
To attain that will be a supreme delight
He is all the time pressing forward with keen expectancy
There are many hopeful aspects of the situation
The situation is greatly improved
May we have a part in bringing in a new and better day

PATRIOTIC

The new patriotism
The golden age of the federation of the world
A world-wide democracy
A United States of the world
A world patriotism
A universal alliance
A league of peace
A glorious future for the nations of the world

Pessimistic

Universal democracy
A supreme court of arbitrament
A peace federation
The end of autocracies
The end of secret diplomacy
It is subversive of every principle of our democracy
Pan-Americanism
Pan-Germanism
International patriotism
A democracy as broad as humanity
International federation
The new prosperity
One of our chief claims to glory is

PESSIMISTIC

I found myself under my juniper tree
It is the very mystery of perversity
He is in a woeful state of mind
A sense of desolation
There came upon my heart an intolerable burden of despondency
A dreary conclusion
The unexpected and adverse strokes of fortune
A damper on my hopes
A gloomy consolation
A discouraging moment

Friendless, homeless, hopeless, undone
Impossible of accomplishment
Grave symptoms
A forlorn hope
A nameless foreboding
One has to be optimistic to find anything hopeful in the present outlook
A somber and mournful aspect
A sign of ill omen
He has the habit of dating existence by the memory of its burdens
A sea of trouble
Under the pressure of calamity
A welter of sordid interests
A very flood of wretchedness
A sorry plight
Moments when one grows sick of mankind
Inexpressibly miserable
A very gloomy report
He is etching the black pictures deeper and deeper into his consciousness
By some strange fatality
Hearts bursting with despair
A terrible legacy
With a groan of sickening remorse
With a sense of desolation
Many vicissitudes
All true in a finished civilization

Political

He has seen many a bitter day of sorely tried hopes
The many accessories of evil
Crushed by burdens
The misspent strivings of mankind
Errant human nature
To move in paralyzing dread
Man is born to trouble as the sparks fly upward
A particularity which converts every trifle into a thorn
A dark and stormy sea

POLITICAL

An unworthy piece of legislation
An odious piece of class legislation
A grave indictment of independent citizenship
Names of genuine weight on the roster of delegates
Signs of a genuine awakening in the nation
Deliberate malfeasance in office
A flagrant offense against public opinion
Indulging simply in pure buncombe
Log-rolling schemes
A public disgrace
A blaze of popular resentment
Political fakery

Blind partisanship
An unfortunate deadlock
Public apathy
Under the old régime
In the initial days of the campaign
A shifty self-seeking politician
Astute diplomats
A corrupt public sentiment
From long association with politics
The real state of affairs in the nation
The last word of political wisdom
The pressing questions of the hour
Facts officially winked at
Recreant to a solemn trust
A sincere desire to safeguard the public
Refreshing to the people
Close to the heart of affairs
Hesitating at no extravagance
These recriminations go on endlessly
An era of good feeling
For political advantage
Scrupulously avoiding any offense against his party
One of the most prominent and potential among the leaders of his party
One cannot blame him for being resentful when the organ of his party flouts and ridicules him

Prudential

He is quick to anticipate the veerings of public taste

It is regarded as a mere eczema on the body politic

The engrossing questions of the day

We must set ourselves to hunt out helpful policies

PRUDENTIAL

By careful discrimination

It must be handled with gloves

Every statement carefully weighed and checked

Without any undue haste

For prudential reasons

I have added a decent little amount to my small income

Under strict and precise supervision

It takes some trouble to ascertain the facts

I do not mean to hamper myself by any fine-spun theory

By a most conservative estimate

With superior prudence and foresight

He really should be more cautious

The precaution necessary to insure safety

With due caution

I would advise caution

Precautions have been taken

RIDICULE

I have tried to read him without skipping
Wonderful to relate
Growing beautifully less
Painful occasions
Not worth the powder to shoot him
A trifle dull
He devotes himself to leisure with much assiduity
A bit of femininity
He is never troubled with a serious thought
The slightest modicum of common sense would teach that
One half humbug and the other half hypocrisy
Very material tastes and ambitions
He is committing literary assault and battery on somebody whose works he has not read
Pretty playthings
The frivolous gabble of women
Fanciful pipe-dreaming
There is no activity within his cerebral cavity
A toy avalanche
He sniffed scornfully
He watched the proceeding from the seat of the scornful
One or two notches short of perfection
Confess you have dreamed this
After the wont of his kind

Satisfaction

The one and only man who knows what to do
and how to do it
He is romancing
Possible but still improbable
Too sanguine
Too eager
Unfortunate venture
Small talk

SATISFACTION

It is so satisfying
I had the secret satisfaction of
I was wonderfully pleased with it
With great satisfaction
Complete satisfaction
An unmixed satisfaction
Quite content in almost anyone's company
It is ample reward for the hardships endured

SUSPICION

A lurking suspicion all the while
A chronic distrust
An uncertain sense of something hidden
Timid misgivings
In such a way as to raise a mild suspicion that
Inclined to be suspicious

TERSE

Snoozed
Villainous
A ninny
Hob-and-nobbing
In hunks
A snack
Good form
Chit-chat
Crisscross and catercornered
Glib-tongued
Gilt-edged
Sly digs
Cold cash
Snap judgment
Far-fetched
Topsy-turvy
Human acorns
Ear-kissing arguments
Poking fun

III

Phrases for Clergymen and Religious Workers

Blessings

BIBLE PHRASES—Blessings

Who giveth us richly all things to enjoy, I Tim. vi., 17.

He will ever be mindful of his covenant, Ps. cxi., 5.

He filleth thee with the finest of the whcat, Ps. cxlvii., 14.

He satisfieth the longing soul, Ps. cvii., 9.

He that toucheth you toucheth the apple of his eye, Zech. ii., 8.

He shall feed his flock like a shepherd, Isa. xl., 11.

As the heaven is high above the earth so great is his mercy toward them that fear him, Ps. ciii., 11.

He filleth the hungry soul with goodness, Ps. cvii., 9.

He healeth the broken in heart, Ps. cxlvii., 3.

He is kind to the unthankful, Luke vi., 35.

Thanks be unto God for his unspeakable gift, II Cor. ix., 15.

As the shadow of a great rock in a weary land, Isa. xxxii., 2.

The desert shall rejoice and blossom as the rose, Isa. xxxv., 1.

Clergymen

The God of truth, Isa. lxv., 16.
The blessing of the Lord it maketh rich and he addeth no sorrow with it, Prov. x., 22.
The steps of a good man are ordered by the Lord, Ps. xxxvii., 23.
Blessed shall be thy basket and thy store, Deut. xxviii., 5.
In every thing give thanks, I Thess. v., 18.
I have a goodly heritage, Ps. xvi., 6.
A feast of fat things, Isa. xxv., 6.
The promise of eternal inheritance, Heb. ix., 15.
His soul shall dwell at ease, Ps. xxv., 13.
Thy sleep shall be sweet, Prov. iii., 24.
More precious than rubies, Prov. iii., 15.
The peace of God which passeth all understanding, Phil. iv., 7.
With joy unspeakable and full of glory, I Pet. i., 8.
Underneath are the everlasting arms, Deut. xxxiii., 27.
Let us put on the armour of light, Rom. xiii., 12.
More than heart could wish, Ps. lxxiii., 7.

BIBLE PHRASES—Hope

Prisoners of hope, Zech. ix., 12.
Heir of all things, Heb. i., 2.
We are saved by hope, Rom. viii., 24.

The eye of the Lord is upon them that hope in his mercy, Ps. xxxiii., 18.

Which hope we have as an anchor of the soul both sure and steadfast, Heb. vi., 19.

We are perplexed, but not in despair, II Cor. iv., 8.

Thou shalt be secure because there is hope, Job xi., 18.

The children of promise, Gal. iv., 28.

He hath given everlasting consolation and good hope through grace, II Thess. ii., 16.

Hope to the end, I Pet. i., 13.

From strength to strength, Ps. lxxxiv., 7.

He staggered not at the promise of God, Rom. iv., 20.

BIBLE PHRASES—REDEMPTION

Though your sins be as scarlet they shall be as white as snow, Isa. i., 18.

The forgiveness of sins, according to the riches of his grace, Eph, i., 7.

As far as the east is from the west so far hath he removed our transgressions from us, Ps. ciii., 12.

A bruised reed shall he not break, Isa. xlii., 3.

Like as a father pitieth his children so the Lord pitieth them that fear him, Ps. ciii., 13.

I will refine them as silver is refined, Zech. xiii., 9.

Clergymen

In whom we have redemption, Eph. i., 7.

Now unto him that is able to keep you from falling, Jude 24.

Not by works of righteousness which we have done, but according to his mercy he saved us, Titus iii., 5.

Moved with compassion, Matt. ix., 36.

Partakers of the divine nature, II Pet. i., 4.

Mighty to save, Isa. lxiii., 1.

Look unto the rock whence ye are hewn, Isa. li., 1.

The wrath of man shall praise thee, Ps. lxxvi., 10.

Wise unto salvation, II Tim. iii., 15.

A man after mine own heart, Acts xiii., 22.

The redemption of our body, Rom. viii., 23.

Love covereth all sins, Prov. x., 12

The truth shall make you free, John viii., 32.

Love suffereth long and is kind, I Cor. xiii., 4.

Unto the pure all things are pure, Titus i., 15.

The eyes of your understanding being enlightened, Eph. i., 18.

I keep under my body, and bring it into subjection, I Cor. ix., 27.

Justified from all things, Acts xiii., 39.

One God and Father of all, who is above all, and through all, and in you all, Eph. iv., 6.

He hath made us accepted in the beloved, Eph. i., 6.

BIBLE PHRASES—Work

Zealous of good works, Titus ii., 14.
Labor of love, I Thess. i., 3.
Rich in good works, I Tim. vi., 18.
Fellowhelpers to the truth, III John 8.
Doing the will of God from the heart, Eph. vi., 6.
That with well-doing ye may put to silence the ignorance of foolish men, I Pet. ii., 15.
Laying up in store for themselves a good foundation against the time to come, I Tim. vi., 19.
The laborer is worthy of his hire, Luke x., 7.
A pattern of good works, Titus ii., 7.
We are laborers together with God, I Cor. iii., 9.
I will very gladly spend and be spent for you, II Cor. xii., 15.
Let all things be done decently and in order, I Cor. xiv., 40.
The sleep of a laboring man is sweet, Eccl. v., 12.
Their nobles put not their necks to the work, Neh. iii., 5.

BIBLE PHRASES—Warning

The lust of the flesh, and the lust of the eyes, and the pride of life, I John ii., 16.
The tents of wickedness, Ps. lxxxiv., 10.

Clergymen

Abomination to the Lord, Prov. xi., 20.
Whatsoever a man soweth, that shall he also reap, Gal. vi., 7.
Let the wicked forsake his way, and the unrighteous man his thoughts, Isa. lv., 7.
His enemies shall lick the dust, Ps. lxxii., 9.
The way of transgressors is hard, Prov. xiii., 15.
Fools make a mock at sin, Prov. xiv., 9.
By thy wrath are we troubled, Ps. xc., 7.
At their wit's end, Ps. cvii., 27.
A perpetual reproach, Ps. lxxviii., 66.
Blind guides which strain at a gnat, and swallow a camel, Matt. xxiii., 24.
He that hath ears to hear let him hear, Luke xiv., 35.
Yet will I not leave thee wholly unpunished, Jer. xlvi., 28.
The wicked are like the troubled sea, Isa. lvii., 20.
The axe is laid unto the root of the tree, Luke iii., 9.
Lewd fellows of the baser sort, Acts xvii., 5.
They have sown the wind, and they shall reap the whirlwind, Hosea viii., 7.
Worse than an infidel, I Tim. v., 8.
A man of unclean lips, Isa. vi., 5.
As he thinketh in his heart so is he, Prov. xxiii., 7.
Terrible as an army with banners, Solomon's Song vi., 4.

Warning

Wise in their own eyes, Isa. v., 21.

No weapon that is formed against thee shall prosper, Isa. liv., 17.

The way that leadeth to destruction, Matt. vii., 13.

Punished with everlasting destruction from the presence of the Lord, II Thess. i., 9.

The last state is worse than the first, Luke xi., 26.

The wages of sin is death, Rom. vi., 23.

Outer darkness, Matt. viii., 12.

Be sure your sin will find you out, Num., xxxii., 23.

The unfruitful works of darkness, Eph. v., 11.

For we can do nothing against the truth, but for the truth, II Cor. xiii., 8.

Past feeling, Eph. iv., 19.

Admonish him as a brother, II Thess. iii., 15.

And others save with fear, pulling them out of the fire, Jude 23.

Eternal judgment, Heb. vi., 2.

That ye may consume it upon your lusts, Jas. iv., 3.

A great gulf fixed, Luke xvi., 26.

In the bond of iniquity, Acts viii., 23.

Whited sepulchres, Matt. xxiii., 27.

When I begin, I will also make an end, I Sam. iii., 12.

Clergymen

BIBLE PHRASES—UNCLASSIFIED

An everlasting foundation, Prov. x., 25.
More precious than of gold that perisheth, I Pet. i., 7.
The power of the grave, Hosea xiii., 14.
The people of God, Heb. xi., 25.
An ornament of grace, Prov. i., 9.
The peaceable fruit of righteousness, Heb. xii., 11.
The righteousness of the law, Rom. viii., 4.
The law of sin and death, Rom. viii., 2.
The light of life, John viii., 12.
Good tidings of good, Isa. lii., 7.
The tongue of the wise, Prov. xv., 2.
The Prince of peace, Isa. ix., 6.
The counsellors of peace, Prov. xii., 20.
The firstfruits of all thine increase, Prov. iii., 9.
A goodly heritage, Ps. xvi., 6.
The good fight of faith, I Tim. vi., 12.
The paths of the Lord, Ps. xxv., 10.
The secret of the Lord, Ps. xxv., 14.
The courts of our God, Ps. xcii., 13.
A diadem of beauty, Isa. xxviii., 5.
Before the foundation of the world, Eph. i., 4.
Everlasting habitations, Luke xvi., 9.
A faithful creator, I Pet. iv., 19.
Lord thou hast been our dwelling place in all generations, Ps. xc., 1.

Unclassified

He shall have dominion also from sea to sea, Ps. lxxii., 8.

The eternal God is thy refuge, Deut. xxxiii., 27.

God is the strength of my heart, Ps. lxxiii., 26.

The joy of the Lord is your strength, Neh. viii., 10.

A crown of glory that fadeth not away, I Pet. v., 4.

Unsearchable riches, Eph. iii., 8

A crown of righteousness, II Tim. iv., 8.

Ever learning, and never able to come to the knowledge of the truth, II Tim. iii., 7.

Let thy words be few, Eccl. v., 2.

There is no discharge in that war, Eccl. viii., 8.

A living dog is better than a dead lion, Eccl. ix., 4.

Wizards that peep, and that mutter, Isa. viii., 19.

He smelleth the battle afar off, Job xxxix., 25.

While I was musing the fire burned, Ps. xxxix., 3.

In the valley of decision, Joel iii., 14.

For who hath despised the day of small things, Zech. iv., 10.

To the law and to the testimony, Isa. viii., 20.

A covenant with death, Isa. xxviii., 15.

Absent in body, but present in spirit, I Cor. v., 3.

Fallen from grace, Gal. v., 4.

Clergymen

The refuge of lies, Isa. xxviii., 17.
Line upon line, Isa. xxviii., 13.
Carried about with every wind of doctrine, Eph. iv., 14.
Let every man be fully persuaded in his own mind, Rom. xiv., 5.
Great plainness of speech, II Cor. iii., 12.
Prove all things; hold fast that which is good, I Thess. v., 21.
A book of remembrance, Mal. iii., 16.
The law of kindness, Prov. xxxi., 26.
A mother in Israel, II Sam. xx., 19.
The land of the living, Ps. cxvi., 9.
I am escaped with the skin of my teeth, Job xix., 20.
A still small voice, I Kings xix., 12.
His eye was not dim, nor his natural force abated, Deut. xxxiv., 7.
Let me die the death of the righteous, Num. xxiii., 10.
A soft answer turneth away wrath, Prov. xv., 1.
Not of the night, nor of darkness, I Thess. v., 5.
An understanding heart, I Kings iii., 9.
Hide me under the shadow of thy wings, Ps. xvii., 8.
A word fitly spoken is like apples of gold in baskets of silver, Prov. xxv., 11.

Unclassified

Establish thou the works of our hands, Ps. xc., 17.

Whose I am, and whom I serve, Acts xxvii., 23.

This is a faithful saying, and worthy of all acceptation, I Tim. i., 15.

Her children arise up, and call her blessed, Prov. xxxi., 28.

Their folly shall be manifest to all men, II Tim. iii., 9.

Lest I should be exalted above measure, II Cor. xii., 7.

They have sold a girl for wine, Joel iii., 3.

In your patience possess ye your souls, Luke xxi., 19.

Eyes full of adultery, II Pet. ii., 14.

Every idle word that men shall speak, Matt. xii., 36.

My speech shall distill as the dew, Deut. xxxii., 2.

A strong consolation, Heb. vi., 18.

Great treasure and trouble therewith, Prov. xv., 16.

A lover of hospitality, Titus i., 8.

A wholesome tongue, Prov. xv., 4.

Not greedy of filthy lucre, I Tim. iii., 3.

A cheerful giver, II Cor. ix., 7.

The children of light, I Thess. v., 5.

Speaking the truth in love, Eph. iv., 15.

The sword of the spirit, Eph. vi., 17.

Clergymen

The tree of life, Prov. iii., 18.
The wings of the wind, Ps. xviii., 10.
A crown of life, Rev. ii., 10.
Not weary in well doing, Gal. vi., 9.
Invisible things, Rom. i., 20.
Slow to wrath, Jas. i., 19.
An everlasting sign, Isa. lv., 13.
The hidden things of dishonesty, II Cor. iv., 2.
A thorn in the flesh, II Cor. xii., 7.
A cloud of witnesses, Heb. xii., 1.
The day is far spent, Luke xxiv., 29.
As one having authority, Matt. vii., 29.
Borne the burden and heat of the day, Matt. xx., 12.
A word spoken in due season, Prov. xv., 23.
Words of truth and soberness, Acts xxvi., 25.
Mighty in word and deed, Luke xxiv., 19.
Not grudgingly or of necessity, II Cor. ix., 7.
Faithful unto death, Rev. ii., 10.
Incorruptible and undefiled, I Pet. i., 4.
The mind of Christ, I Cor. ii., 16.
I obtained mercy, I Tim. i., 13.
The words of truth and soberness, Acts xxvi., 25.
This is the finger of God, Ex. viii., 19.
By the law is the knowledge of sin, Rom. iii., 20.
Things that accompany salvation, Heb. vi., 9.
If a man die shall he live again? Job xiv., 14.
Watchman, what of the night? Isa. xxi., 11.

In the furnace of affliction, Isa. xlviii., 10.

Owe no man anything, but to love one another, Rom. xiii., 8.

A wounded spirit who can bear, Prov. xviii., 14.

Riches certainly make themselves wings, Prov. xxiii., 5.

A man to have friends must shew himself friendly, Prov. xviii., 24.

Whoso findeth a wife findeth a good thing, Prov. xviii., 22.

It is more blessed to give than to receive, Acts xx., 35.

Perfect love casteth out fear, I John iv., 18.

A good name is rather to be chosen than great riches, Prov. xxii., 1.

The spirit truly is ready, but the flesh is weak, Mk. xiv., 38.

Comfort one another with these words, I Thess. iv., 18.

Of whom the world was not worthy, Heb. xi., 38.

DEVOTIONAL

Enable us to meet with gentleness and forbearance any opposition to our wishes

And when we shall have fulfilled thy purposes concerning us on earth may we be received into the everlasting mansions revealed to us through Jesus Christ our Lord

Clergymen

Fortify us by Thy spirit against the temptations that await us

May the sweet influences of the Gospel gladden and redeem many hearts

Rule thou in our hearts

Fill us with holy thoughts and noble desires

May we be warned of sin and its dreadful consequences

We thank Thee for the rich promises and precious hopes of the Gospel of Thy Son

We would breathe into Thine ear our gratitude for mercies so free

May our hearts glow with a renewed sense of Thy love

Fulfill in us Thy gracious promises

Help us to cherish the heavenly disposition of Jesus Christ our Lord

Scatter the darkness from our minds by the beams of thy heavenly truth

Teach us how to attain that holiness which will make us holy like Thee

Clothe us with all social and domestic graces

Help us to discharge our debt to the world

Daily we would supplicate Thy mercy and protection

Make our duties plain before us

May we be inflexible in every good purpose

Unseal our spiritual vision

We pray for those who are languishing on beds of sickness and have wearisome days and nights assigned them

We are sorry that we are so fondly attached to the things that perish

Encompass our minds this day with thoughts of heaven

Wilt Thou take us unto Thy keeping this day

Pity our frailities

Inspire us with an abiding gratitude

In the defenseless hours of sleep Thou hast preserved us

With the light of another morning we would lift our hearts to Thee in grateful acknowledgment of thy goodness

Suffer not our ears to become dull to the cry of misery

May no day pass without thy blessing

May our hearts be open to the glad tidings

Keep us from distrustful thoughts

Give us a cheerful and unfailing confidence that Thou art at the heart of affairs

May our trials be borne with Christian meekness

May our difficulties work out for us some spiritual good

Encourage us in every right endeavor

May the thought that Thou seest us check every wrong motive and evil impulse

Give us calmness and self-control under every
disappointment and provocation
Fulfil in us thy gracious promises
Fill our hearts with thy rich grace
Soften our sorrows
Grant us thy reviving grace
Fill us with thy perfect love
Cheer saddened hearts
In our spirits sweetly move
Sanctify our deep distress

HALLOWED

God of All Love
Lord God Almighty
Our Heavenly Father
Our Gracious God
Our Father
Almighty and Most Merciful God
O Thou Guardian of our lives
Father in heaven
Divine Father
Most Holy and Most Merciful God
All-Merciful Father
Eternal and Ever-Blessed God
Almighty God our Father
Eternal and All-Wise God
Father of All Mercies

Arraignment

God of All Love
O God, Almighty and All-Holy
O Righteous Father
Father of Infinite Love
O God, Father of Lights
Most Glorious and Eternal God
Father of Mercy and God of all comfort
O Lord God of Infinite Excellency
O Thou Great Shepherd
Our Gracious Lord
O Glorious God and Savior
Most High and Mighty God
Our Father and our God
O Thou All-Bountiful Giver
O Matchless Son of Man
O Savior of Mankind
O Holy and Ever Blessed Spirit
O Spirit Divine

SERMON PHRASES—Arraignment

The hollow shams and conventionalities of our day
No adequate sense of His holiness
Baser than a beast
No keen and poignant perception of sin
The lessening sense of sin
His own heart as cold as frost

Clergymen

Sad and sinful days
Our hearts hot with wrath and indignation against sin
Evil to its core
The devil's signet
Of decidedly earthly passions
All dried up in one's soul
Lust was kindled in his heart
Base, mean, prudential, paying no tribute to the Divine excellence
The parching blight of sin
Beware of artful, designing persons
Sins come in groups, in battalions
Like the frosts of sin which blight the sweet blossoms of youth
And taste the tang of the bitter cup
The hundred and one enemies of our peace, comfort, and efficiency
The burning poison in his veins
There is nothing more likely to betray a man into absurdity than
It vexes, grieves, thwarts, repels, drives off the Spirit of God
Beware of the beginnings of sin
Over head and ears in debt and drink
The peril of riches
A coronet of shame
The secret beginnings of sin

Arraignment

By so doing, he is sowing the seed of a fatal
infection
Trifling with great spiritual realities
Lest it might lead to things undesirable
The horror of a bottomless pit
Habits which quietly sap the foundations of
life
Words which will shock some dainty soul
A sickening devotion to the pursuit of wealth
The evils of unrighteousness in civic life
It seems to contradict the designs of Providence
A narrowing effect on the conscience of those
who have embraced it
Care lest one be inveigled into perdition
Words which ought to make us twinge
Words of worldly wisdom
A brewing storm of hostility
The world's hardest battlefields of sin and sorrow
In their hearts the feuds of ages
A wretched, dejected, sin-blasted soul
Carnality in the heart
The great enemy of mankind
The black enormity of sin
A miserable grudge in your heart
The spawn of the evil one
A heritage of hate
A dauntless worldling
From whose very touch one's delicacies shrink

Clergymen

The fires of a sensitive religious experience no longer glow
The grip of evil forces
All alarming, all hateful, all detestable
A gnawing sense of condemnation in the heart
Those who abuse God's great gift of speech
Some of these enormities put to blush heathenism itself
These are the new Dark Ages
No deeply seated opinions of right and wrong
A state of lazy indifference
Apparently destitute of ambition
Worthy neither of respect nor honor
Soft and easy days
Mean, petty, social prejudices
The temptation to fritter away life in interests that are small and mean
Everlasting confusion
The enemy shall come in like a flood
The man that speaketh froward things
The resurrection of damnation
A rebellious house
God resisteth the proud
The works of darkness
Unstable as water
Spreading himself like a green bay-tree
The words of his mouth were smoother than butter but war was in his heart

Consecration

Seest thou a man wise in his own conceit?
There is more hope of a fool than of him
An unprofitable servant
His mouth is full of deceit and fraud
The wicked boasteth of his heart's desire
A sad vocation
A heart of adamant
A hardened cynic
The vain things
The enormity of sin
A scoffing world
A defeated one
Tenements of dust
The jealous eye
The everlasting burning
The hell of hate
A despicable heart
A sullen silence
A disdainful glance
A brittle promise
A sorry specimen

SERMON PHRASES—CONSECRATION

All there is of us for God
Willing to take a lowly place anywhere to serve God
There is a constancy of spirit that beats like the pulse of God

A heart full of longing to live in a larger way
The hardships and joys of a life of toil
My heart is set to do all the will of God
A fervent and vigilant life in the service of God
Men and women who are living beautiful lives of sanctified service
A work in which every man may bear a share
The depth and fervor of our belief
To lay our tribute at the feet of one who is nobler than the noblest
Perfect abandon unto the will of God
Not much engaged in cumbering affairs
Into spheres of sublime service
In harmony with His character
The free-will offering of our lips and purses
Men who tried to stem the flood-tide of sin
In fearless pioneering
In plucky unyielding struggle with evil
In unapplauded toil among the poor

SERMON PHRASES—Hope

When the human heart sings with rejoicing hope
When smiles begin to chase the tears
A real breath of heaven
With radiant face
A draught of heavenly pleasure
A triumphant hour

Insight

A lively sense of exultation
The dove of peace sings in our hearts
I begin to discover somewhat of His beauty
Transported with joy
A current of pure and hallowed joys flowing through the channels of the heart
An intense inner happiness
A most happy glimpse into the things of God
Secret essences which turn life into a garden of unspeakable delights

SERMON PHRASES—INSIGHT

He put his finger on the nerve
A very delicate discernment
Point it out very tenderly
A shrewd, acute man of the world
God will set you aside if you do that
With the discerning eye of faith
A complete revelation of the inner life
Face to face with the purposes for which we were created
A fire which consumes the dross
Foregleams of the mercy that would save the blackest sinner
A deep knowledge of the things of God
The delicate hand of a discerning nurse
Far more exacting in its demands
Submitted to the arbitrament of merciless justice

SERMON PHRASES—INVITATION

The Lord grant that we may possess his grace
I am wonderfully glad that
Thank God for the better impulse to
How passing strange it is that
I covet earnestly God's blessing upon us
God grant that we may be wise
May the eternal and unspotted life of blessedness infix itself in us
Make no delay
The very God of peace establish you
May we yield our affections to God's control
Seek help from the Mighty One
Turn not away your ear
He will uphold, bless, satisfy you
Seek the sweet grace of Jesus
You must know Redemption's theme
God does not leave us to our discretion
It is not an easy matter for God to save a sinner
God would woo us into heavenly fellowships
God has poured out a wealth of affection upon us
Believe that God is behind what you say for him

SERMON PHRASES—JOY

Brighten up the corner where you are
Every cloud will wear a rain-bow if your heart keeps right

Joy

The nameless responsive thrill of something deep
within us
A treasure better than gold
Pleasures pure and lasting
Heaven's eternal spring
The song lifting its pæan out of the night
In the sweetest fellowship
Strains that sweetly soothe
The exquisite little joys of life
An atmosphere of tranquillity
A new-found joy
Tears of joy and gratitude
Joy which flows like a river
In joyful anticipation
With joyful enthusiasm
Possibilities of which we hardly dreamed
The sweet melodies of heaven
The great glad tidings
The glory of his grace
The sweetest name on earth
The blissful refuge
A balm for the weary
The very friend you need
The priceless gems of God's book
A joy divine
Songs of sweetest praise
A triumphant hope
Thrones of love

A heaven of love
The kingdom of light
The fullness of his blessing
The life-giving stream

SERMON PHRASES—Kindness

Sympathies as wide as the world
A sensibility as tender as it is refreshing
Wider sympathy
Of cosmopolitan sympathies
Poverty-stricken in his sympathies
World-wide sympathies
A great soul
The very heart of kindness
Diffusing the gospel of kindliness
The employments of active benevolence
Full of kindly deeds
The milk of human kindness
A stray word of kindness
Kinder than the kindest
With utmost gentleness
Of gentlest sympathy
Of a kind and forgiving disposition
They exchanged mutual assurances of continued good will
The secret of contented and fruitful living

Love

The staple interests and occupations of the common life
Heaven and earth brought into strange accord
An unembittered disposition
The sign of God-like charity
Slow to speak ill of any one
Beautiful in the eyes of fond affection
A heaven of love in your heart
A wonderfully kind heart
Members of a forgiving family
Sweet in disposition
Glorifying God in the common round
The gracious inclination of the will
The outcome of a rich experience

SERMON PHRASES—Love

He's the great heart-maker
Winsomely and lovingly
The sacrifices of love
Matchless kindness
Unwavering love
A redeeming love-energy
A glad service of love
A legacy of love
A flame of sacred love
The sweet kingdom of God's love
The wondrous story of God's love

The wonderful words of life
The genial flame of affection
The marvel of His love
The love that conquers
Love divine, all loves excelling
The glorious sense of the Divine right of love
Made beautiful by Divine love
The warm yearning intimacy of God's love
The sweet and unpolluted flower of love
The richest joys out of heaven
If our bosom burns with the fires of love
Love that translated us from alienation to family favor
Love, pure, warm, and changeless
Songs of redeeming love
An eye of love
A heaven of love
Abounding love
With undiminished love
Love is the universal language
What the world needs is love

SERMON PHRASES—MANLINESS

The sanctifying love of a strong victorious man
A patient, loving, uncomplaining soul
A clear-eyed seer of the things of God
An uncompromising foe of evil

Manliness

Sagacious in spiritual things
A mind full of vigorous hopeful uplifting thoughts
He has a wonderful experience of grace
He passed through the fires of affliction
He is a graduate of the University of Difficulty
We are resolved to lay no stumbling-blocks in the way of the progress of the redemption of the world
We have the abiding consciousness that we are fundamentally right with God
He is in the apostleship of spiritual beauty
A great lover of mankind
He takes a living, loving interest in men
Moral worth
Resolved not to depart from the channel of truth
Holy in character
A warmth of temperament
Generous impulses
The imposing grace of a noble self-restraint
A chaste refinement of spirit
Splendid reserve power
Well content to go down to the grave unpraised
Taking steps toward the threshold of heaven
Walking in the blessed path of peace, power, and purity
A nobility of life
Worthy of more attention than it has yet received

A worthy friend
Hands full of character and delicacy
With unfaltering lip and heart

SERMON PHRASES—REDEMPTION

Washed white from crimson sins
The process of becoming perfect
The right temper of the soul
The Divine hostility to sin
Brought into saving relationship
The ultimate purpose of redemption
A redeemed fellowship
The dynamics of the redeemed life
In God's eternal economy
The Divine method of doing things
The splendors of redeeming grace
The unspeakable humility of Calvary
An eternal redemption
The mysteries of redemption
A wealth of unveiled glories
Rich in sanctity, wisdom, and redemptive power

SERMON PHRASES—SALVATION

Hearts sensitive to His presence
Sweet with the perfume of God's breath
A spotless splendor that holds us in fascination

Salvation

To them that nestle down into his will, God is like a mother
All the loving links that bind us to heaven
The psalm of adoring lip
The ceaseless exercise of reverence
Tokens of His favor
In those lofty moments when the soul is near God
The riches of His great grace
The river of rare and exquisite delights
In the highest realms of aspiration
A treasury of golden thoughts
Elements which have the luster and preciousness of pearls.
Kept from the entanglements of sin
A heart made pure and right
The unforgetable memories of a pure home
The purest of the pure
A way of fortifying one's soul
Moment by moment I'm kept in his love
Steadfast in the strength of God, and true
The free and kindly intimacies of the fireside
The fair realities of the sanctified life
The peaceful atmosphere of good will
Make a covenant with your eyes lest sin get into your heart
We must get corruption out of the heart for one never knows how it will betray

Enabled to act continually with integrity
Free from narrow and selfish motives
The grand truths of redemption
The news of mercy
The mighty Sacrifice
The sons of peace
The paths of peace
The heavenly steeps
The life-giving stream
The glory of holiness
The well-spread table
The river of regenerating energy
A joy-giving truth
The sacred longing of the soul
The enduring brotherhood
A new ideal of plenty
A beautiful faith
The eternal spirit

SERMON PHRASES—Sorrow

Burdens pressing down upon head and heart
A feeble lonely soul
Heart longings
A picture of despair
A life of struggle, grief, and pain
With inexpressible longings
A struggling heart

Sacred

The appalling darkness of Gethsemane
The lonely way of isolation
On a beach of wrecks
He walked with bleeding feet the flinty path
A figure of woe fit to melt the most obdurate heart
The struggling myriads of the poor
The noble army of martyrs
Like a sad and poignant refrain
The roots of bitterness

SERMON PHRASES—SACRED

An infinitely loving and all-wise heart
Worthy to receive endless praise
Far up the everlasting hills in God's own light
The hallowed beauty of the eternal God
The glorious outlines of His holiness
The pure pellucid waters of His grace
Illumined by the indwelling of eternal light
The presence of the most high God
The all-wise and gracious counsels of God
The unshadowed depths of eternal holiness
The adoration of the eternal
A celestial melody
In resplendent glory
In the mountains of God
The great and blessed God who inhabits eternity
The unblemished holiness of heaven

Clergymen

SERMON PHRASES—Victory

The hour of opportunity
It teems with the virile life of rugged men
An aggressive moment
One transcendent moment
An insatiable thirst for knowledge
With loving urgency
On the victory side
I was splendidly heartened by
Into the large and beautiful realm of the spirit
The word of magnificent promise
A mastery of the obscure problems of life
The full current of Divine power
Expanding the social ministry of Jesus
A fine swinging step born of a happy confidence
A profound and refreshing satisfaction
The reckless joy of the Lord

SERMON PHRASES—Unclassified

Love-compelled
Idle-scorning
Heavy-laden souls
Redeeming grace
Kind designs
Mutual burdens
Plentiful redemption

Unclassified

Eternal councils
Spiritual penetration
Gracious surprises
Pure delight
Transforming grace
Toilsome years
Impure ambition
Spiritual progress
Spiritual confusion

IV

Phrases for Letter-Writers

FOR LETTERS OF CONDOLENCE

Be assured of my deep sympathy with you in this time of great sorrow

I know too well that words cannot comfort you

Trusting that you will see the bright side of the dark cloud—I am with deep sympathy your friend

How can I attempt to comfort you in the bitter affliction which has befallen you

Would there were more like——

I regret to hear of your continued indisposition and hope that before long you may return to your wonted good health

A sweet and uncomplaining spirit

I should rejoice if I could be with you

I can only send my sympathy and best wishes for your speedy and complete recovery

Courage—hope remains

Time will heal many heartaches

May the Father of Mercies give you the rich consolation of His grace and preserve and strengthen you for your family

May you be sustained in this most bitter trial

May you live in the confidence that —— is in the enjoyment of everlasting happiness

With a prayer for every blessing on yourself,

Affectionately your friend.

It is a great comfort to us that

Words are inadequate to express my feelings

There are times when one cannot express himself in written words

The pen refuses to express adequately my sympathy to you

I sympathize keenly with you in the loss of your excellent

They are not lost to us

God will surely give you a kindly guidance in this hour of trial

The intimations of a future life shall some day be realized and we shall see and know again those whom we have "loved, and lost awhile."

Many beautiful traits made up his character

I join with you and his other friends in mourning his death most sincerely

It shocked me very much

I have heard with the greatest distress of

I had learned to have a very warm feeling for

I had been intimately enough associated with him to feel that I knew him very well

I know that your heart must be sorely grieved

God shall overcome this King of terrors

It is written, "As thy days so shall thy strength be"

We expect to see our loved ones in happier, brighter worlds above

God is able to soothe and sustain the distressed soul

May God's love shine more and more in our hearts until the day breaks and the shadows flee away

His name was never mentioned in public without the most tender regard

He careth for you

A stronghold in the day of trouble

A covert from the storm

We unite in sending our love and sympathy

With warm regards

We beg you to accept our commiseration

Our hearts sorrow with you

He is such a very great comfort to us

We are uplifted by the assurance that

A light which sorrow cannot quench

We must all wait the call of God with a calm trust

Let me have the comfort of hearing from you

The hand of God has been heavy

Letter-Writers

We must live in the blessed anticipation of the glory that is to come
Do not fear, for God knows what is in your heart
Your path seems full of thorns
Your weather is bleak, but the storms will cease
Your sky is dark, but the sun shines
May the Everlasting Arms sustain you in the flood of sorrow
May God comfort you
Out of the thorn springeth the rose
I know you are in grief and heaviness
We commend you to the mercy and grace of God
The bitterness of affliction
The present floods of sorrow
You will have to cast your anchor in the dark
May your heart be constant
The Lord will surely give you rest from the days of adversity
I would that you should always have the sweet experience of the consolations of God
We all have the good will of Him who dwelt in the bush
My heart is heavy for you
We must wait till the fair morning of the resurrection
I write my blessing, earnest prayers, the love of God, and the sweet presence of Christ to you and yours

Cast thy burden upon the Lord
Thou hast known my soul in adversities
I know their sorrows
A refuge from the storm
A shadow from the heat
In the furnace of affliction
I will hedge up thy way with thorns
Tribulation worketh patience
Our light affliction
In all their affliction he was afflicted
He healeth the broken in heart
For a small moment have I forgotten thee but with great mercies will I gather thee
God that comforteth those that are cast down comfort you
We shall have to bear our crosses with meekness and patience
So good a friend is capable of making any calamity light
The great loss you have sustained has caused me much uneasiness
I know not how to express my sorrow at the news which I have just received
That God may give you great consolation under this heavy burden is my fervent prayer
I should be glad if I could suggest anything to lighten your trouble and make your path a little more smooth and easy

The grateful sense of your kindness will never be erased from my mind

If my services can in any way assist you do not hesitate to ask for them

I am sincerely sorry to hear of your loss

He carried the riches of God within himself

He was a royal-hearted man

We are greatly afflicted by the melancholy intelligence which reached us that

I knew the sterling integrity of his character

May God breathe into your heart peace and cheerful resignation

My mind is filled with very grateful memories

He was greatly beloved

I fall back upon a very delightful verse of Scripture: "He is able to subdue all things unto himself."

My heart is filled with the deepest gratitude as I think of

We send our earnest wishes for your speedy recovery

My most affectionate regards to

You seem to have your full share of human vicissitudes

He had such a fund of courage and good cheer

Dear, sweet, loving mother

A letter replete with tenderness and affection

Such a sad circumstance has come to you
Your sorrow's night
When one's heart is unspeakably tender
We extend our heartfelt sympathy
In your hour of trial
She was such a beautiful character, loved by every one
In these lonely hours you must not be cast down for there is help from God
His Word says that they that wait upon Him shall renew their strength
She was God's good angel in your home
Grief that saps the heart
I account you mine
His name will long linger in our household
We must be brave in the face of trying circumstances
Of gracious memory
She bears up with the utmost fortitude
I received the melancholy intelligence last evening that
He was the kindest, and most generous of men
The sweet remembrance of the just
A workman that needeth not to be ashamed
If God be for us who can be against us
Of whom the world was not worthy
Whom the Lord loveth he chasteneth
Let not your heart be troubled

All things work together for good to them that love God

A bruised reed shall he not break

Many daughters have done virtuously but thou excellest them all

It is better to go to the house of mourning than to the house of feasting

He giveth his beloved sleep

A very present help in trouble

We took sweet counsel together

God will take us into their goodly company some glad day

Glimpses of the reality which we instinctively feel will sometime be ours

The unmeasured things of hope which God has prepared for men

Our lives we must humbly commit to the guiding hand whose blessing we adore

Filled with strong consolation

There are many avenues by which God would come in and richly bless us

He had the secret of keeping the sacred fires aglow

He knew the deep principles of experimental religion

Ordinary consolations do not avail us

He knew the secret of beautiful living

He was a silent witness of right living

Many admiring friends
One who ministered so carefully and tenderly
All the more tragic because
And this thought will be our comfort that
Of gentle presence
All the gentle virtues came into full blossom
Looking forward with a Christian's bright anticipation of a glad reunion
Persisted in keeping mind and spirit on the sunny side of life however hard the trials and difficulties
Mother's fortitude and hopefulness is a lesson to us all
We send our united and sincere condolences
The news of your painful loss has been a great surprise to me
I have read of your bereavement with the deepest sorrow

FOR LETTERS OF THANKS

I am sending this letter as the silent messenger of my thanks and good wishes to you
I must find some way to make due acknowledgment of your goodness to me
I trust I may be able to do you some service, that I may be worthy of your kind approbation

I will not write more but wait until a better opportunity enables me to more fully express myself

Please allow me to send my most thankful acknowledgments for the favor you have conferred upon me

I know not how to express my grateful thanks for your

The grateful sense I have of your kindness will never be erased from my mind

I take this first opportunity to send you my thanks for

You have exceedingly obliged me by

I beg to acknowledge, with thanks, the receipt of

I am grateful to you for your kind expression of sympathy

Though your kind letter has waited so long for a reply, you may be assured that I was not unmindful of its messages of sympathy

Please accept my warmest thanks for your kindness

I am deeply indebted to you for

I received your very agreeable letter, and hasten to give you my most hearty thanks for your

I thank you for your hospitality

We had a most delightful time while with you. Please accept this little memento of our regard

CONCLUDING CLAUSES FOR CHRISTMAS LETTERS

I send you tender tidings of regard this Christmas Day

I hope you will lack nothing to make a Merry Christmas

On this day I think of you, and wish you happiness without limit

May all joys combine to give you a happy Christmas Day

With best wishes and heartiest greetings for Christmas

I wish you a joyful Christmas from the bottom of my heart

With kind remembrances and all good wishes for a Merry Christmas and a Bright New Year

With best wishes for a Merry Christmas and a New Year of health and happiness

The best of good wishes for a happy Christmas

May Christmas bring you plenteous store of happiness and joy

Heaps of Christmas wishes

With the kindest thoughts and the best of good wishes for a happy Christmas

I heartily send all good Christmas wishes to you and yours.

CONCLUDING CLAUSES FOR NEW YEAR LETTERS

May this New Year turn out to be the happiest and the best

With best New Year wishes

May all your plans and wishes come true in this New Year

A happy New Year

May the New Year be a happy year for you

A joyous New Year

With all best wishes for a splendid New Year

With all the kindest wishes for good health and good fortune throughout the year

With my most hearty greetings and sincere good wishes for you for all the coming year

With best wishes for a year of great blessing

May the New Year be full of the kindliest benedictions

With kind wishes for a year of the brightest prospects

V

Phrases for Writers and Public Speakers

Introductory Clauses

INTRODUCTCRY CLAUSES

I am credibly informed that
I respectfully decline to take any part in
I did not think fit to remonstrate
I could not be but favorably disposed toward a people
It struck me forcibly
I consider their action most reprehensible
You must often have remarked that
I confess it is not without trepidation that
I am not disposed to think that
I saw how thoroughly he was duped
It was clear to me that
I was struck dumb by
To my inexpressible delight
I had little inclination to
I have no less an authority for the statement than
The trouble with us poor mortals is
From my personal point of view
I note with satisfaction that
I cannot help suspecting that
I have generally observed that
I have many choice recollections of
I had the good fortune to be

Writers and Public Speakers

You will hardly credit it but
It frets my soul to see
I am desirous of establishing some kind of a relationship between
He works on the assumption that
I forbear to enter into the minute particulars of
I am thankful to have been the means of
I throw this out as a good subject of
What I was going to observe was
I am always deeply and vividly impressed by
I am ready to guarantee that
I have been fortunate enough to
I assert without fear of successful contradiction that
I am free to admit that
I have repeatedly urged that
I am most heartily in favor of
I have carefully inquired into the
It is immaterial to me whether
I am constrained to think that
I will not let such a remark go unchallenged
He is conversant with the situation
I have now ample cause to affirm that
He took up the cudgels in favor of
Have you never been struck with the similarity between
I will hazard the observation that
I am convinced that in his heart he

Introductory Clauses

If it be true, as is predicted, that
It is a matter of the simplest demonstration that
The apparently inevitable conclusion is that
It is self-evident that
It is a very rare occurrence that
We cannot resist the conviction that
It can fairly be suspected that
For obvious reasons there are
It is nothing less than amazing to find that
A marked example of similar tendencies is to be found in
In view, therefore, of
It goes without saying that
It will be noted that
To an extent probably never known before the
There is little reason to anticipate that the
Nevertheless, a large number fail to understand the perfectly obvious conclusion that
After allowing for all probabilities and possibilities we find that
This was largely due to the fact that
It is remarkable that
We have a comfortable conviction that
It cannot be without significance that
A safe rule to observe is
A startling possibility is
There is ample assurance that
The wonder of wonders is

Writers and Public Speakers

The program here suggested is grounded in the conviction that
The primary requisites of
Allowing something for the possibility of error we
And it should not be forgotten that
It is worthy of remark that
This is essentially a time for
The evidence is overwhelming that
Nothing is more fallacious than
We must rectify the errors of
It is poor policy to
It is interesting if true
It is strikingly illustrated by
It does not matter how improbable the prospects may be
It is an error that leads to the most pernicious consequences to imagine that
It is universally conceded that
On the whole it is amusing to find that
The most interesting phase of the situation is
It is significant that
As a matter of fact
It will be remembered that
There can be no two opinions that
It cannot be maintained that
Even so, it is only a question of
It is interesting to note that
The redeeming feature of it all is

Introductory Clauses

Very likely the explanation lies in the fact that
While it is understood that
His point is not germane to the subject
There are some who go instinctively to the bottom of any matter
At all events
To put it tersely
It is too late to lament the
The argument is not so convincing to the modern mind
The prime reason for
Ordinary prudence would suggest that
Every mother's son of us will follow suit when
It is not for me to dictate but simply for me to suggest that
It is well within the bounds of conservative statement to state that
Many desirable reforms would be accomplished if
How much faster the chariot of progress would advance if
How many struggling little enterprises would gain a solid underpinning if
It is rather a nice point whether
This will lead us by the shortest cut to the conclusion that
It is beyond all contradiction a more happy situation than can ever be promised by

Writers and Public Speakers

If we are to make a fair show in the world we must
This is not an uncommon kind of prejudice
A very vital equation in the problem is
The antecedent probability is
The argument is thoroughly convincing if
The incontrovertible evidences are
There is something wholesome in all of this if
There is always something to admire if
There is no mistaking the qualities which
It was nothing short of a crime for
In these days it is refreshing to see
And has it come to this that
There is little chance of
There is no longer any doubt that
It may be maintained with equal plausibility that
It might be worse if
We have cause for profound satisfaction in that
What a splendid thing it is to be able to say that
It is the acme of folly to
It is indispensably necessary that
The conclusion cannot be escaped that
It is idle to speculate on the outcome of
It was clearly apparent that
It is extremely necessary that
It is pretty good evidence that
It has been proved that

Introductory Clauses

It was found that
It is yet to be demonstrated that
It is out of the question to
If the truth were known
There is no gainsaying the fact that
A pity it is that
The crucial question is
Excuses are not reasons, therefore
It comes as a refreshing surprise to learn that
It is utterly unbelievable that
One of the great outstanding features of
It goes without saying that
An unusual amount of discrimination is demanded in
However that may be, we
Notwithstanding the fact that
It is virtually certain that
It is surprising how
It is chronicled that
It seems eminently fitting that
It is imperative that
From a narrow notion of human duty men imagine that
Who has not remarked the readiness with which the
We should be devoutly thankful for
We are willing to go to any reasonable length if
Well has it been said that

Writers and Public Speakers

It is sterling sense to
It is worthy of remark that
They will hardly have the effrontery to deny that
It transpires, as many suspected, that
One of the most significant items was
It is not enough that
It is a fact of tremendous significance that
The advantages are so manifold that
These facts amply confirm the opinion that
One of the unavoidable sources of
Almost anything might have been expected from
Despite all this the
It is true that
The notable feature of it all is
It is hardly too much to say that if
It is barely possible that
It is absolutely useless to expect that
Incidentally, it is interesting to observe that
This does not mean, however,
In view of the assertion that
Persistent efforts are being made to create the impression that
There can be no question that
The entire system is founded upon the recognition of the soundness of the contention that
There never has been a time in our history when

Introductory Clauses

Few persons will question that if it had not been for
It is time that
It is rank foolishness to think that
And it may be noted that
This condition is due in large measure to the fact that
It is hardly possible that
Men have frequently fancied that
To the rightly perceiving mind it would appear that
A little reflection will easily convince anyone that
It is remarkable that
Little hope is cherished that
No secret is made of the fact that
It was anticipated that
The opinion has been everywhere expressed that
In the event of
In other words
Furthermore
Notwithstanding
Nevertheless
These words are not a little surprising because
One can hardly go astray in believing that
On the whole
For after all

Writers and Public Speakers

It is not outside the realm of possibility that
We have no doubt whatever that
In fact, we are in a position to state that
It is still an open question whether

VI

Happy Combinations

HAPPY COMBINATIONS

Genuine gratification
Unmixed approbation
Conspicuous examples
Highly creditable
Beautifully attired
Exquisite fitness
Unfailing variety
Extremely vague
Boon companions
Substantial benefits
Manifold iniquities
Conflicting accusations
Tender sensibilities
Unquestioning faith
Fawning praise
Languid dullness
Egregious blunders
Perverse antipathies
Quite superfluous
Weak-based impressions
Inexhaustible resources
Crude civilization
Inadequate treatment

Happy Combinations

Pleasant conceits
Daring speculations
Too intricate
Exalted principles
More pliable
Augured evil
Mutual fidelity
Fine qualities
Implicit confidence
Hard facts
Ample opportunity
Rightly named
Apparent misfortune
Deep-rooted convictions
Drastic counsel
Hardly decent
Painfully prevalent
Ulterior designs
Fine enthusiasm
Homely simplicity
Petty malice
Irritating trifles
Special fondness
Mental elasticity
Various foibles
Frank delight
Speechless misery
Strong and deep-rooted beliefs

Happy Combinations

Capital sport
Untrammeled self-expression
Utter destitution
Untutored judgments
Rigid economy
Wide celebrity
Solid reasons
Over-strained authority
Profoundly influential
Exorbitant prices
Sound economics
Extremely prepossessing
Cold calculations
Fanatical opposition
Swashbuckling heroes
Exceptionally good
Acutely sensible
Doubly striking
Quite frequently
Impressive language
Practically impossible
New-fangled notions
Highly desirable
Idle dreams
Legitimate desires
Directly involved
Gross injustice
Unrelaxing care

Happy Combinations

Capricious ways
Splendid enterprise
Shattered hope
Hot indignation
Honied flattery
Parental regrets
Flimsy finery
Loose thinking
Social cohesion
Vast ideals
Mental slovenliness
Refined perceptions
Primary thoughts
Gracious thoughts
Willful exaggeration
Unnecessary unkindness
Sadly lacking in tender and generous sentiments
Foolish and pernicious talk
Most reprehensible
Downright rudeness
Sentimental inanity
Positively asinine
A poor cheap, tawdry business
In an abysmally inferior way
The most intolerable nuisance
The basest treachery
Utterly futile as well as mischievous
Utterly inadequate

Happy Combinations

Palpably unjustified
Wholly unauthorized
Utterly ineffective
Absolutely immaterial
Persistently hostile
Woefully mistaken
Notoriously unreliable
Altogether obtuse
Mentally incapacitated
The sum of all villainies
Unutterably wearisome
A piece of stupid management
Picayunish prudence
Absolutely inexplicable
Cold facts
Militant hostility
Arrant nonsense
Invincible ignorance
Domestic felicity
Lucid explanation
Thoroughly wholesome
True inwardness
Decidedly handsome
Remarkably fine
Officious prognostications
Prodigiously stupid
Respectable alliances
Sanguine views

Happy Combinations

Frequent opportunities
Judicious praise
Absolutely unnecessary
Amiable qualities
Unquestionably advantageous
Hearty concurrence
Peculiarly becoming
Awkward circumstances
Remarkably pretty
Highly agreeable
Supercilious nonsense
Sorely tried
Dauntless perseverance
Social obligations
Grandly simple
Halting expediency
Absolute frankness
Countless irritations
Great compensations
Worth while
Pious reflections
Ill tidings
Strong temptations
Basal energies
Unsuspected wealth
Flat blasphemy
Utter insufficiency
Gross negligence

Happy Combinations

Financial distress
Sincerely unpretentious
Conspicuous ability
Prim propriety
Invariably practiced
Haphazard thoughts
Lasting acquisitions
Shrewd guesses
Rare sagacity
Snugly ensconced
Quite apathetic
Dilettante tastes
Blunting drudgery
Foundation beliefs
Irksome tasks
Drooping spirits
Charming surprises
Radiant hopes
Instinctive delights
Discontented days
Inherent dislikes
Cool courtesies
Surpassing merits
Particularly opprobrious
Joyously happy
Uncannily quiet
Very sparingly
Indubitable facts

Happy Combinations

Abundant opportunities
Collateral causes
Sterling truth
Extravagant conjectures
Sedulously watching
Almost invariably
Unmistakable evidence
Sound judgment
Laudable purposes
Neatly arranged
Beautifully clean
Ample proofs
Sane judgment
Remote horizons
Headstrong youths
Well-matured convictions
Excessive loquacity
Contributory negligence
Overweaning pretensions
Blind blunders
Obsequious servants
Genuinely glad
Keen reproach
Nimble-minded
Adroit questioning
Absolutely refused
Highly educated
Above mediocrity

Happy Combinations

Ready wit
Of inestimable value
Truly admirable
Filial reverence
Gross unfitness
Greater efficiency
Sober memories
Intense protestation
Flagrant violation
Scathing criticism
Thoroughly ingenuous
Official primacy
Perfectly asinine
Instinctive delight
Rigidly orthodox
Utterly worthless
Unproved assertions
Approximate results
Ill-concealed contempt
Reckless speculation
Measureless eras
Grateful acknowledgments
Signal benefactions
Widespread traditions
Rival claimants
Superabounding liberality
Scrupulous care
Distinctive features

Happy Combinations

Altered circumstances
Serious complications
Grievous troubles
Striking illustrations
Turbulent times
Graphic descriptions
Conclusive evidence
Vehement denunciation
Tame and prosaic
Obstinate resistance
Utterly unreliable
Graceful selfishness
Due consideration
Utterly incredible
Maligned and misrepresented
Fickle and irresolute
Consummate skill
Specious pretenses
Atrociously bad
Singularly appropriate
Prayerful meditation
Well-authenticated testimony
Comparatively modern
Strong conviction
Wretched poverty
Athletic prowess
Intrinsic worth
Unblushing disobedience

Happy Combinations

Pernicious practices
Intrinsic interest
Puissant efforts
Deleterious influences
Nice distinctions
Broad discriminations
Social amenities
Nicely married
Well disposed
Well-bred
Well-connected
Foolish energies
Useless retrospection
Injurious impressions
Dangerous propensities
Dark prejudice
Long-cherished opinions
Impartial judgments
Merciless exposure
Lavish expenditure
A clinching appeal
A ready response
Of deepest import
A powerful inducement
A sober judgment
A well-worn theme
A trustworthy account
A commercial instinct

Happy Combinations

An impassive spectator
An unassuming manner
A cruel absurdity
A pernicious tendency
A rare accomplishment
A constructive program
An acquired taste
A wide acquaintance
A practical impossibility
A complete overhauling
A disturbing influence
A sharp emergency
An urgent warning
An itching palm
A carnal desire
A perilous sleep
An imposing appearance
A vicious circle
A prodigious curiosity
A mendacious statement
A disastrous slump
A well-grounded prejudice
An inextricable dilemma
A noble way
A drawn struggle
A bold control
An inexcusable fault
A serious annoyance

Happy Combinations

A grave fault
A contemptible misanthropy
An irreducible minimum
A negligible quantity
An easy explanation
A counter irritant
A base intruder
A conservative bias
A healthy reaction

VII

Sample Letters

CONDOLATORY

MY DEAR ——,

We were exceedingly sorry to learn of your bereavement. There are many whom we have "loved and lost awhile." But God will take us into their goodly company some glad day. We unite in sending our sincere sympathy.

With warm regards,

MY DEAR ——,

We are greatly afflicted by the melancholy intelligence which has reached us that —— is no more with us. He carried the riches of God within himself, and was a royal-hearted man. He was greatly beloved by all of us. With a prayer for every blessing on yourself,

Affectionately, your friend,

MY DEAR FRIEND,

It is with great regret that we learn of the sad occurrence at your home. Please accept our united and sincere condolences.

With deepest sympathy,

REPLY TO CONDOLATORY

MY DEAR ——,

I am very grateful for your kind expression of sympathy. My heart is filled with gratitude when I think of my good friends.

Sincerely yours,

MY DEAR ——,

I thank you kindly for your consoling letter. Though I have waited some time to reply, its messages were none the less deeply appreciated.

Your friend,

THANKS

MY DEAR ——,

I am sending this short note as a silent messenger of my thanks to you. I had a most delightful visit at your home.

Cordially yours,

MY DEAR ——,

Please allow me to send my most thankful acknowledgments for the favor you have conferred upon me. I trust I may be able some time to do a service for you.

Sincerely yours,

Word Index

Index

WORD INDEX

A

B

C

Index

Index

Index

Index